Cambridge

Elements in
editec
Robert Kennedy
University of California, Santa Barbara
Patrycja Strycharczuk
University of Manchester

COARTICULATION IN PHONOLOGY

Georgia Zellou
University of California, Davis

CAMBRIDGE
UNIVERSITY PRESS

CAMBRIDGE
UNIVERSITY PRESS

University Printing House, Cambridge CB2 8BS, United Kingdom

One Liberty Plaza, 20th Floor, New York, NY 10006, USA

477 Williamstown Road, Port Melbourne, VIC 3207, Australia

314–321, 3rd Floor, Plot 3, Splendor Forum, Jasola District Centre,
New Delhi – 110025, India

103 Penang Road, #05–06/07, Visioncrest Commercial, Singapore 238467

Cambridge University Press is part of the University of Cambridge.

It furthers the University's mission by disseminating knowledge in the pursuit of
education, learning, and research at the highest international levels of excellence.

www.cambridge.org
Information on this title: www.cambridge.org/9781009077330
DOI: 10.1017/9781009082488

© Georgia Zellou 2022

First published 2022

A catalogue record for this publication is available from the British Library.

ISBN 978-1-009-07733-0 Paperback
ISSN 2633-9064 (online)
ISSN 2633-9056 (print)

Coarticulation in Phonology

Elements in Phonology

DOI: 10.1017/9781009082488
First published online: July 2022

Georgia Zellou
University of California, Davis

Author for correspondence: Georgia Zellou, gzellou@ucdavis.edu

Abstract: There is debate about how coarticulation is represented in speakers' mental grammar, as well as the role that coarticulation plays in explaining synchronic and diachronic sound patterns across languages. This Element takes an individual-differences approach in examining nasal coarticulation in production and perception in order to understand how coarticulation is used phonologically in American English. Experiment 1 examines coarticulatory variation across sixty speakers. The relationship between speaking rate and coarticulation is used to classify three types of coarticulation. Experiment 2 is a perception study relating the differences in realization of coarticulation across speakers to listeners' identification of lexical items. The author demonstrates that differences in speaker-specific patterns of coarticulation reflect differences in the phonologization of vowel nasalization. Results support predictions made by models that propose an active role by both speakers and listeners in using coarticulatory variation to express lexical contrasts and view coarticulation as represented in an individual's grammar.

Keywords: sound change, coarticulation, phonology, phonetics, individual differences

ISBNs: 9781009077330 (PB), 9781009082488 (OC)
ISSNs: 2633-9064 (online), 2633-9056 (print)

Contents

1 Introduction

Coarticulation is phonetic variation due to the overlap of adjacent articulatory gestures. For example, to produce the word "bean," the nasal gesture needed for the final /n/ begins early in the preceding vowel. We focus on anticipatory nasal coarticulation, since this type of coarticulatory variation is common across languages that have nasal consonants (approximately 98% of the world's languages have a nasal consonant in their inventory, according to the *World Atlas of Language Structures*, Maddieson, 2013) and in every language with nasal consonants, some amount of coarticulatory vowel nasalization has been observed in production (Hajek, 2013). However, the theoretical backdrop of the current work, as well as the implications of the findings, are relevant for thinking about coarticulation more broadly. Coarticulation is a natural property of speech, and, in fact, necessary for fluent production. From an articulatory perspective, coarticulation is gestural overlap of phoneme units during speech production. Thus, coarticulation results in contextual variation in the realization of phoneme units. Coarticulatory variation is natural and ubiquitous, since it is an inevitable consequence of the influence that articulating one sound has on another (speech sounds are rarely produced in isolation!). However, there is ongoing debate and discovery about how coarticulation is represented in the mental lexicon of speakers. Furthermore, from a diachronic perspective, the pathway of CVN > CṼN > CṼ is a common historical change (Chen & Wang, 1975; Hajek, 1997). The goals of the present work are to (1) cover the key empirical and theoretical concepts relating to coarticulation, (2) demonstrate a laboratory phonological approach toward exploring and understanding patterns of coarticulation by presenting original and novel production and perception data, and (3) discuss the implications of investigating patterns of coarticulatory variation for the field of phonology. More broadly, we seek to examine the role of coarticulatory variation in synchronic and diachronic phonological variation.

1.1 Phonological Explanations for Coarticulatory Variation

One characterization of language is that it is a system that enables discrete elements to be combined in an infinite number of ways, with each combination conveying (or having the potential to convey) a different meaning. This applies to the phonological component of the grammatical system, as with others. For instance, "bed" and "ben" are lexical items composed of the same phonological elements except for the final one. Yet, these words also vary in that additional acoustic-phonetic cues to the final consonant are temporally distributed as coarticulation on preceding sounds. Because coarticulation is a type of context-dependent variation, whereby sounds take on predictable characteristics of other neighboring sounds, it might be viewed as not relevant to encoding information critical to contrasting between lexical items. For instance, some theoretical approaches aim to minimize phonetic-articulatory information that is stored in the underlying forms of words (Jackobson et al., 1952; Chomsky & Halle, 1968). In approaches such as these, the "idiosyncratic" information (i.e., minimal amount of symbolic-featural information that makes the word distinctive) and "systematic" information (i.e., contextually predictable details) hold different statuses in the grammar (Kenstowicz & Kisseberth, 2014). For a word like "ben," the idiosyncratic information consists of the minimum amount of phonological detail that allows "ben" to contrast with the other legal word of English. Since there is no pair of words [bɛn] and [bɛ̃n] that contrasts in nasalization on the vowel alone in English, these models assume that coarticulatory information is not stored: since coarticulation is predictable, it is classified as a type of systematic information that can be implemented post-grammatically. Thus, since coarticulatory nasality is noncontrastive (since it does not encode information critical to discriminating between words like "bed" and "ben"), such a perspective might assume that its implementation in production is less important and less careful (perhaps weaker or more variable, etc.) than phonetic details directly located on the contrastive sound. Similarly, some have assumed that the perception of coarticulatory patterns is also not critical, or even that its presence could lead to perceptual confusion if it is not factored out or ignored by the listener: the acoustic consequences of the nasality might just make the vowel sound "bad" (i.e., less like the canonical oral version of the vowel) and thus harder to interpret (Lahiri & Marslen-Wilson, 1991).

More recent work, however, has shown that many noncontrastive properties of speech sounds are stored as well. In particular, research taking an experimental approach to phonological variation have explored how some properties related to the temporal implementation of phonemes are learned. An example of such an approach is Cho and Ladefoged (1999) who conducted a cross-linguistic survey of the phonetic implementation of voice onset time (VOT) in plosives across different place of articulation contrasts. They observed that differences in the temporal realization of VOT across languages are arbitrary. Since these temporal patterns were not consistent across languages and could not be tied to a strictly biomechanical explanation, Cho and Ladefoged concluded that such details had to be specified in speakers' grammar as learned aspects of the phonetic representation of sounds. On the other hand, other aspects of the temporal realization of VOT, specifically, variation across place of articulation, were found to be consistent across languages and could be linked to an articulatory explanation. Their demonstration led them to argue for two levels of phonological encoding: a level containing segment contrasts (e.g., minimally specified phoneme units) and a level containing language-specific phonetic values that are assigned to articulatory gestures (see Cho & Ladefoged, 1999, figure 10). In addition, automatic and universal articulatory implementation processes also apply during speech production, determined by physiological and aerodynamic processes. Thus, this approach demonstrates that precise experimental analysis can inform which phonetic differences are "phonological" (i.e., broadly meaning that they reflect learned and controlled variation), compared to those that are "mechanical," thus not represented in the phonological grammar. Similar approaches to that taken in Cho and Ladefoged (1999) have been effective in outlining techniques for proposals about which *coarticulatory* features are physiological in origin and which are deliberate and targeted versus biomechanical aspects of the speech signal. Similar to the Cho and Ladefoged (1999) approach, there is much work demonstrating that patterns of coarticulation are language-specific (Beddor et al., 2002; Cohn, 1990; Keating & Cohn, 1988; Manuel, 1990; Schourup, 1973), indicating that speakers learn aspects of coarticulatory detail in their grammars.

What makes languages differ in coarticulatory features? Many researchers have searched for functional explanations for language-specific coarticulatory patterns. For instance, a prominent hypothesis for cross-linguistic differences in the production of coarticulation is that the system of contrast in a language constrains coarticulation (Manuel, 1990, 1999; Manuel & Krakow, 1984). The proposal is that when there is a lexical contrast to maintain for a particular feature (e.g., vowel nasalization), there will be less coarticulation (i.e., constrained coarticulatory vowel nasalization). For example, in French, vowel nasality is contrastive and encodes differences in word meanings (e.g., *paix* [pɛ] vs. *pain* [pɛ̃]). But noncontrastive coarticulatory nasality occurs in the context of nasal consonants as well (e.g., *peigne* [pɛɲ]) (Cohn, 1990; Delvaux et al., 2008). So oral vowels are nasalized when they occur adjacent to nasal consonants; this means that vowel nasality is both contrastive and noncontrastive in French. Thus, a listener who encounters a nasalized vowel in French has to discern whether the nasality is the result of a contrastively (i.e., phonologically) nasal vowel or an adjacent nasal consonant. In French, then, the fact that vowel nasality is contrastive in the language might limit the realization of anticipatory coarticulation, or might lead to perceptual difficulty or confusion to the extent that it does occur. Indeed, nasal coarticulatory patterns are observed to be less in degree and extent in CVN words in French, relative to that observed in other languages (Cohn, 1990; Delvaux et al., 2008; Montagu & Amelot, 2005). Hence, the differences in the patterns of contrastive and coarticulatory nasality can be viewed as representing perceptually motivated constraints on speakers in French.

However, studies of coarticulatory vowel nasalization in other languages with a nasal vowel contrast have found evidence for extensive coarticulatory nasalization, contrasting with the French case. Yet, they observe that the phonologically nasal vowel versus coarticulatorily nasalized vowel contrast can be maintained in other ways. For instance, Scarborough et al. (2015) examined both coarticulatory and contrastive vowel nasalization patterns in Lakota (a Siouan language of North America). They found that the location and magnitude of the nasalization peak within vowels varied across words in ways that are difficult to account for in biomechanical terms. Specifically, low phonologically nasal vowels in carryover contexts (i.e., with a preceding nasal consonant) exhibited peak nasalization at a late point in the vowel; meanwhile, in anticipatory contexts, the peak was at an early point of the vowel. Thus, phonologically nasal vowels which are in nasal consonant contexts and thus additionally subject to contextual nasality are produced with peak nasalization in the vowel portion furthest away from the coarticulatory source. Furthermore, peak nasalization in these contexts was of a larger magnitude than other phonologically nasal vowels; in fact, it is reported that some Lakota speakers describe the NV~NṼ as one of a "weakly" nasal versus "strongly" nasal vowel (Scarborough et al., 2015, p. 302). One explanation provided was that these variations are deliberate and derive from a system-wide need to keep the contrast between nasal and oral vowels distinct, especially in contexts where coarticulatory nasalization might neutralize that contrast. That native speakers are explicitly aware of the differences in magnitude provides support that this phonetic distinction is perceptible. However, an important point to note from the Scarborough et al. (2015) study was that they report individual variation in this observation: some speakers actually did exhibit neutralization of the NV~NṼ contrast. Thus, there appears to be variation within languages in the extent to which this type of contrast maintenance in nasal consonant contexts applies.

There are many other empirical studies from other languages that provide a nuanced picture of how coarticulatory patterns are constrained by the system of lexical contrast. In fact, there is some work exploring variation in coarticulatory patterns across languages, above and beyond what can be explained by systems of contrast. For example, Huffman (1988) compared degree and timing of nasal coarticulation in Akan (Niger-Congo language, Ghana) and Agwagwune (also Niger-Congo, Nigeria), two languages that differ in the phonological status of vowel nasalization. She found no differences in degree or extent of nasal coarticulation, though there was a difference in where peak nasalization occurred. Furthermore, Farnetani (1990) found nasal coarticulation in Italian to be very restricted, despite the fact that there is no oral-nasal vowel contrast in that language. Aerodynamic analyses of nasal coarticulation in Bininj Kunwok (Gunwinyguan language, Australia) also has shown restricted anticipatory nasal coarticulation, again despite the lack of a phonemic nasal vowel contrast in the languages (Stoakes et al., 2020). Thus, the cross-linguistic evidence suggests that any relation between phonological contrast and coarticulation may not be direct, especially with respect to nasal coarticulation.

A related question is, why is there systematic variation in coarticulation within a language. Some researchers have explored what factors might be relevant in determining within-language variation in patterns of nasal coarticulation. Similar to the Manuel (1990) hypothesis, many researchers have explored functional explanations for within-language coarticulatory variation. Lindblom's body of work, for instance, takes the stance that phonetic variation is adaptive and the relationship between phonological organization and speech output is optimizing. For example, hypo- and hyperarticulation theory (Lindblom, 1990) proposes that articulatory variation reflects a dynamic, real-time trade-off between speaker-oriented and listener-oriented real-time communicative forces. The model proposes that phonetic variation reflects a speaker's dynamic adaptation to communicative pressures. When the listening situation is ideal, the speaker can conserve articulatory effort and produce less effortful hypospeech. Yet, when there is some impediment to communication, the speaker might adapt their speech to be more intelligible to the listener by hyperarticulating. In effect, the H&H model predicts that the dynamic interplay between speaker- and listener-oriented forces in a conversational interaction will influence phonetic variation. Many of H&H theory's predictions have been examined in empirical work on clear speech. For example, speech produced with the explicit goal to be clear exhibits longer segment durations and more peripheral vowel spaces, relative to less clear speech styles (e.g., Bradlow et al., 2003; Moon & Lindblom, 1994; Smiljanić & Bradlow, 2009). Furthermore, as predicted, speech with these phonetic adjustments has been shown to be more intelligible than conversational, or casual, speech (Bradlow & Bent, 2002; Picheny et al., 1985).

Lindblom (1990) makes specific predictions about how *coarticulatory* patterns will manifest in response to trade-offs between the needs of the speaker and the listener. For example, his view is that the default "low cost" form of behavior by the motor system is increased coarticulation since it facilitates low-effort production of adjacent distinct articulations, while listener-oriented hyperspeech might contain reduced coarticulation in order to enhance the unique phonological properties of distinct segments. Yet, Lindblom (1990) does acknowledge that coarticulation might serve perception since it "does provide valuable cues" for the listener (p. 425). Indeed, contrasting with Lindblom, Beddor (2009) posits that since coarticulation is perceptually informative in that it structures the speech signal to provide early and redundant information about the underlying features, it is something that speakers use in a highly controlled manner to provide cues to listeners. The notion that coarticulatory patterns are under speaker control and used to enhance coarticulation in strategic ways to help listeners comprehend and parse the speech signal has support from other work. Scarborough and colleagues (e.g., Scarborough, 2013; Scarborough & Zellou 2013; Zellou & Scarborough, 2015) explore how speakers' patterns of coarticulatory vowel nasalization might be listener-directed in some cases. For example, Scarborough and colleagues have found that speakers systematically vary extent of nasal coarticulation across situations with more or less output-oriented pressures. For instance, in situations where there is an ostensible pressure to make speech more intelligible (e.g., when producing words that are more confusable due to a large number of phono-logical neighbors or in communicative tasks with an interlocutor where there is an authentic pressure to be more intelligible), speakers produce a greater extent of nasal coarticulation than in situations with less intelligibility oriented pres-sures (Scarborough, 2013). Degree of nasal coarticulation on vowels in French may vary systematically depending on neighborhood density, too (Scarborough, 2004). In other words, despite the fact that nasality is completely predictable and incapable of expressing contrastive information in English, and that nasality is contrastive as well as noncontrastive in French, nasal coarticulation is enhanced by speakers of both languages in contexts where CVN words are more confusable, potentially playing a role in perception. Parallel neighbor-hood-conditioned patterns have been shown for nonwords spoken by English speakers (Scarborough, 2012) as well as for other types of coarticulation, namely vowel-to-vowel coarticulation (Scarborough, 2004) and in tandem with other phonetic variables, particularly hyperarticulation (Munson & Solomon, 2004; Wright, 2004) and voice onset time (Baese-Berk & Goldrick, 2009). Thus, conditions where speakers have been shown to enhance primary phonetic cues to phonological contrasts, they also enhance anticipatory coarti-culatory cues to upcoming segments.

1.2 The Role of Coarticulation in Diachronic Change

The fact that different languages exhibit distinct vowel nasality patterns has been the motivation for the development of theoretical models accounting for the role of coarticulatory vowel nasalization in historical phonological change. It has long been noted that synchronic phonetic variation is a precursor to the emergence of innovative sound patterns over time in a speech community (Weinreich et al., 1968). Since coarticulation results in natural and systematic types of synchronic variation in the realization of phonemes, its role in diachronic sound changes has been extensively explored. For instance, coarticulation results in an ambiguous relationship between the speech signal and its phonological structure: [ṼN] could be interpreted as signaling either /VN/ or /ṼN/, or some other possibility, as the intended underlying form. Thus, from the listener's perspective, coarticulation creates a one-to-many (or, many-to-many) mapping between the acoustic signal and the underlying structure of the utterance. The process of a listener "backwards-engineering" the speaker's gestural behavior from the speech signal has been hypothesized to be a mechanism for diachronic sound change (e.g., Ohala, 1993). For instance, Ohala's (1993, inter alia) listener-based model of sound change origins is one prominent proposal for how speech processing mechanisms lead to the phonologization of coarticulation in this way. Ohala argues that listeners generally normalize for coarticulation by ascribing the acoustic effects of gestural overlap to their sources in the speech signal. For nasal coarticulation, this would mean that listeners attribute the vowel nasality in the context of a nasal consonant to its source, and thus analyze that the vowel as inherently nonnasal (e.g., [ṼN] is "reverse-engineered" to /VN/). Evidence for this process comes from work examining how perception of nasal coarticulation depends on context: English listeners hear a nasalized vowel in isolation as nasalized, yet they hear a nasalized vowel in the context of a nasal consonant [NṼN] (Kawasaki, 1986).

However, another possible interpretation of [ṼN] is as /ṼN/. In this scenario, a listener perceives the nasality in the speech signal as an intended property of the vowel and interprets it as reflective of the speaker's underlying representation for that utterance. According to Ohala, in this case, if the speaker's original representation for that utterance was an inherently nonnasal vowel, the listener has "hypocorrected" or "failed" to normalize for the effect of context. The hypocorrection scenario is an event where the underlying representation for a given utterance is different for the speaker and the listener. Such an event has been described as a mini sound change, and accumulation of such situations is hypothesized to be the origin of long-term changes in production targets for speech sounds. However, listeners' sensitivity to coarticulatory variation on sounds in context have been demonstrated in many studies of "partial" perceptual compensation (e.g., Beddor & Krakow, 1999; Fowler, 2005). For instance, Beddor and Krakow (1999) use vowel discrimination tasks where listeners hear two versions of an NVN lexical item, differing only in the presence of nasality in its vowel: one token contained a nasal vowel and the other contained an oral vowel. Participants' responses in discriminating between vowels that contain nasalized vowels in context are above chance, indicating that some coarticulatory effects routinely remain perceptible by listeners (Beddor & Krakow, 1999; Krakow & Beddor, 1991). This is evidence of "partial" compensation for coarticulation and it is argued that sound change might arise via phonologization of this residual coarticulation.

Partial compensation for coarticulation as a potential sound change mechanism has been recruited to explain many common sound changes observed in connection with vowel nasalization. For example, nasalization of vowels results in an acoustic-perceptual lowering of F1 (Krakow et al., 1988). A listener might misattribute the lowered acoustic center of gravity due to the spectral properties of nasality not to the source nasal lowering gesture, but instead to a raised tongue position (which would also lower F1). Thus, the acoustic ambiguity of nasalized vowels presents opportunities for sound change. Indeed, low vowels with nasality are perceived by listeners as higher than oral low vowels (Krakow et al., 1988; Wright, 1986). Furthermore, speakers systematically produce distinct oral articulations for nasalized vowels (both contrastively and coarticulatorily nasalized) relative to nonnasalized counterparts in many languages (Carignan, 2014, 2017; Carignan et al., 2011). This has been argued to reflect the phonologization of distinct oral and nasal vowel qualities that originated in the misattribution of nasalization effects as tongue height variations (Carignan et al., 2011). The effects of nasalization on perceived vowel height can explain historical vowel changes that occur in nasal consonant contexts, such as the raising of /æ/ in CVN words that is found in many varieties of English (e.g., Boberg & Strassel, 2000).

Another mechanism for sound change in the classic Ohala model is hypercorrection. Another speaker, whose representation perhaps reflects previous phonologization of the acoustic effects of nasalization (i.e., someone who has phonologized CVN as /CṼN/), produces an acoustic signal that more closely resembles their intended utterance: [CṼN]. Yet, the listener might make the same assumption for correction, that the nasality is the result of mechanical coarticulatory processes and not intended by the speaker. Thus, the listener might attribute these features to the adjacent nasal coda, "over-correcting." In this case, the speaker's intended representation of the utterance (with a deliberately nasalized vowel [CṼN]) and the listener's interpreted representation of the utterance (with an oral vowel, since they have subtracted the nasality in the signal as due to mechanical processes [CVN]) do not match. There is some empirical evidence that such a process occurs (although it is less well examined than hypocorrection). For example, Harrrington et al. (2013) found that listeners compensated less for coarticulation in unstressed vowels, which they interpret as an instance of hypercorrection. In this case, the speaker's intended representation of the utterance and the listener's interpreted representation of the utterance also do not match, like hypocorrection, yet the listener has normalized for coarticulation to a greater extent than the speaker intended. One of the phonological implications of over-normalization is that it could lead to dissimilatory sound changes. It is interesting to note that changes involving hypercorrection are much less often explored in the sound change literature (a question that is open to be explored in future work).

Ohala's model frames the mechanisms for sound change as resulting from "misperception." This assumption has been questioned by recent researchers examining sound change and revised models of phonologization of coarticulation have been proposed that address these points. In particular, Beddor's (2009) model of a coarticulatory pathway to sound change relies on many of the same assumptions as the previous model, with some important modifications. Beddor (2009) views coarticulation as perceptually useful information, emphasizing the importance of anticipatory nasal coarticulation in providing early cues to the listener to help comprehend the speech signal. For example, anticipatory nasalization can be used by the listener, just by hearing [bĩ], to identify that the word is "bean" not "bead" (Beddor, 2015; Beddor et al., 2013; see also Zellou & Dahan, 2019). Thus, Beddor's model assumes listeners routinely use coarticulatory detail as part of the process of efficiently comprehending the speaker's message.

Furthermore, Beddor (2009) integrates both the speaker's and the listener's roles in explaining how synchronic variation might lead to sound change. For example, coarticulatory variation is a product of speaker-controlled deliberate trade-offs in production. This was examined in a production study of American English words with ṼNC sequences (such "bent" and "bend") where the nasal consonant typically shortens (or deletes) before a final voiceless oral coda. Yet, she observed that while there was variation in the duration of the nasal segment, the total temporal extent of nasalization remains identical across words like "bent" and "bend" indicating the speakers are actively maintaining the duration of nasalization present across these words. Even further, Beddor (2009) argues that the speaker deliberately maintains the velum-lowering gesture even when a shorter gesture might be less effortful. Thus, Beddor (2009) frames this as both grammatical and perceptually oriented: speakers are strategic by realigning the onset of nasalization so that the same amount of that cue is present in the acoustic signal even if it is temporally or spatially realigned. Beddor (2009) links both speaker-controlled and listener-oriented nasal coarticulatory patterns to sound change. Under such a speaker- and listener-driven sound change view, patterns of nasal coarticulation are a learned part of the phonetic structure of the language, used by speakers in strategic ways and the object of close attention by

listeners. Indeed, listeners are highly sensitive to the acoustic effects of coarticulatory nasalization in discriminating lexical contrasts in English. For
instance, Ali et al. (1971) found that when a final nasal or nonnasal consonant
was spliced out from a monosyllabic word, listeners could reliably predict the
missing segment.

Thus, Beddor (2009) proposes that listeners' veridical attention (i.e., sensitivity to coarticulatory details) to the speech signal gives rise to sound changes.
Specifically, she hypothesizes that perceptual equivalence between the multiple
possible interpretations for a given utterance, both within and across individuals, is the mechanism for sound change. This was demonstrated when she
looked at the perception of ṼNC sequences with manipulated temporal extent of
nasal coarticulation. She found that listeners, when rating words manipulated to
vary in the relative duration of the nasalized portion of the vowel and the nasal
consonant, attend to the total sum of nasality duration across a syllable, rather
than the extent of nasality localized on one particular segment. Hence, listeners
do accurately hear information about nasal coarticulation present in the acoustic
signal; but due to the ambiguous relationship between the speech signal and the
multiple possible underlying gestural mappings, listeners have multiple options
to decide on the intended utterance. Thus, variations in the alignment of the
nasalization gesture can lead to perceptually equivalent realization – the listener's choice in selecting which representation reflects the acoustic signal might
lead to variants that are then emphasized by listener-turned-speakers. In this
case, veridical perception of coarticulatory details is not misperception, rather
since there are multiple possible and appropriate interpretations for a given VN
sequence, listeners' choices are not "wrong" (see also Lindblom et al., 1995,
who reframe hypocorrection as an adaptive mechanism that is sensitive to
semantic and situational factors), but reflect differences in the relative weighting across listeners of coarticulation as a cue to word perception.

Another model that revisits and extends some of the hypocorrection model
ideas is Blevins' (2004) model of sound change typology. Blevins also views
synchronic phonological variation as partially reflective of historical sound
change. In particular, Blevins looks for explanation in typological patterns:
the fact that some phonological alternations are common and others are rare
can be explained in terms of how likely or not a respective sound change is to
occur. Blevins' typology emphasizes understanding the aerodynamic, acoustic
articulatory, and perceptual motivations for sound change. Blevins (2004)
argues that sound change is a result of the nature of linguistic representation.
For instance, Blevins assumptions about lexical storage are based on exemplar
models (Pierrehumbert, 2002, 2016). Blevins (2015) argues that the proposal
that lexical representations include memory traces of words with experienced

phonetic detail means that the grammar "is neither purely synchronic nor diachronic: grammars are constantly changing systems, changing ever so slightly each time a new linguistic experience of hearing or speaking takes place, and changing in a myriad of ways as memories themselves wax and wane" (p. 3). Blevins (2004) proposes three types of mechanisms for phonologization, based on different phonetic origins: "choice," "change," and "chance." "Choice" is a way to account for how articulatory variation related to decisions about speech production; for instance, speakers vary their speech as a function of speaking style, along the hyper–hypo speech continuum, can result in phonetically hyper- or hypoarticulated variants that can be the source of novel acoustic variants experienced by listeners. "Change" accounts for perceptual reanalysis, similar to Ohala's hypocorrection mechanisms, whereby a listener hears some property in the acoustic signal that is not an intended feature by the speaker, but interprets it as intended and then this variant becomes the new production target for that listener. "Chance" is where the ambiguity in the speech signal leads to multiple types of phonological interpretations and this one-to-many relationship can lead to variations across listeners in the mapping of the signal to one of the possible forms. With respect to nasalization, Blevins' model accounts for the diachronic change from VN > Ṽ as arising from both articulatory and perceptual factors via "change."

In contrast with Lindblom's adaptive approach to explaining synchronic and historical variation, Blevins does not view all types of sound changes as having an adaptive motivation. Some sound changes, she points out, are "non-optimizing" in the sense that they do not result in a more articulatorily efficient or perceptual distinctive system. For instance, in the phonologization of vowel nasalization, there is an asymmetry where VN > ṼN > Ṽ is more common than NV> NṼ > Ṽ (Kawasaki, 1986; Ohala 1975, Ruhlen, 1978; Schourup, 1973). The asymmetry in patterns such as these can be explained by the interplay of articulatory and perceptual factors (coda weakening is more likely to yield a nasalized vowel with a reduced consonant; anticipatory cues are heard before the causal source), and not an optimizing motivation. Also, Blevins points out that the existence of intra-speaker variability is not consistent with the assumption that phonological systems are inherently optimizing.

Moreover, Blevins discusses one rare sound change that involves the phonologization of multiple levels of vowel nasalization. She describes the phonological system in Palantla Chinantec (Oto-Manguean language, Mexico) where there is an oral/semi-nasalized/nasalized vowel contrast. This pattern, presented in Merrifield (1963) and Merrifield and Edmonson (1999), involves oral vowels contrasting with vowels that can contain two degrees of nasalization: a fully nasalized vowel, where nasalization is initiated early in the vowel, and a vowel with "lighter" nasalization, where nasality is initiated later in the vowel (approximately at vowel midpoint). For one, the observation that the Palantla Chinantec phonological system has a two-level vowel nasalization contrast provides support for the proposal that nonbinary representations for nasalization at the abstract level are possible.

Another relevant point about the Palantla Chinantec nasal system is that it has been proposed that the two vowel nasalization levels are a result of phonologization processes occurring at two distinct points in time. For example, Ladefoged (1971) proposes that the oral~heavily nasalized~light nasalized contrasts are representationally $V \sim \tilde{V} \sim \tilde{V}N$ and that the nasal coda is not realized in the speech signal for the last form. If such a proposal were accurate, this would be an example of the middle stage of the phonologization pathway for vowel nasalization ($VN > \tilde{V}N > \tilde{V}$) as proposed by Ohala (1993) to be present in a language where there was already an oral-nasalized vowel contrast. Furthermore, Merrifield and Edmonson's (1999) acoustic study of eight speakers of Palantla Chinantec reports individual differences: Half of the speakers make the oral~heavily nasalized~light nasalized contrast, while the other half of the speakers produce only an oral~heavily nasalized contrast (three out of eight produce oral vowels in the "light nasalized" condition, and one speaker (reported in a footnote as impressionistic observations) produced heavily nasalized vowels in the "light nasalized" condition).

Phonological models assuming rich phonetic detail stored in representational memory have the benefit of being able to explain both synchronic variation and diachronic change in sound systems. Many recent phonological models allow for mental representations for words that can explain nonbinary, or even gradient, variation within and across languages and over time. Pierrehumbert (2002), for instance, extends exemplar models of representation to lexical storage in order to explain observed phonological variation. Exemplar models propose that linguistic representations are encoded with a vast amount of phonetic detail, gleaned from experiences with words and the contexts in which they are spoken. Thus, memories for words include precise phonetic qualities in which they were perceived, including surrounding lexical context but also details about the speaker and their social properties. However, Pierrehumbert (2016) also allows for abstraction, proposing that the grammar contains an additional layer of representation for types that averages over the cloud of stored phonetically detailed tokens. So, highly detailed representations for individual tokens are stored but grouped together by type (abstract lexical level) allowing for productive phonological and morphological processes. (Recall that Cho & Ladefoged (1999) also propose multiple levels of phonological representation.) Pierrehumbert (2002) provides an explanation for sound change that is based on the nature of lexical representations: phonetic detail from the recorded token of words influences subsequent production and categorization of lexical items, so, as an individual's experience with a word accrues in memory, particular acoustic variants that occurred on that word can bias the exemplar cloud in phonetic space and subsequently lead to a shift in the phonological quality.

In exemplar models of lexical storage, pronunciations of distinct words form nondiscrete, overlapping distributions. Retrieving the meaning intended by a speaker's utterance requires categorical decisions (e.g., the meaning of a given word is either that associated with "bed" or "bend" and cannot be both or something in between) based on an analog signal that provides probabilistic evidence. Identifying words in speech is a process by which people discover which lexical form the speaker must have produced based on the phonetic information. The process of evaluating phonetic information is proposed to be probabilistic because the pronunciation of the same phonological element varies tremendously across speakers, contexts, and instances, and because the same sensory cue can be produced for different phonological elements such as phonemes. Thus, phonological elements are best described as overlapping categories defined over sensory dimensions. Within Bayesian approaches to speech perception, the optimal way to accommodate the many-to-many relationship between sensory cues and perceived elements is to infer the elements that may have given rise to sensory data based on the perceiver's knowledge of the probability distributions associated with relevant perceptual categories, combined with the probability of each element to be uttered generally or in the present context. The view that speech perception is an inferential process computed over probability distributions is gaining prominence in the field (e.g., Kleinschmidt & Jaeger, 2015; McMurray & Jongman, 2011). Empirical findings support such a view: People can reliably rate how well a given sound represents its category (Miller & Volaitis, 1989), demonstrating that people perceive the fine-grained differences between within-category tokens. Furthermore, good category exemplars facilitate the recognition of the word they appear in, relative to poor exemplars (e.g., McMurray et al., 2002). The effects of within-category phonetic details are robust and can be observed on behavioral and physiological measures for several hundreds of milliseconds (e.g., Toscano et al., 2010). Finally, people's categorization of exemplars depends on the dispersion of a category as a whole. Categories with a narrow range of exemplars (i.e., categories for which most exemplars are concentrated within a limited range of values along relevant sensory dimensions) tend to overlap less with one another than categories with a large range of exemplars, thereby reducing the uncertainty associated with the relationship between sensory cues and categories. Clayards et al. (2008) showed that people's phonemic categorization was affected by the dispersion of the distribution they had been exposed to.

There is much work that has asked whether details for coarticulation are maintained over time and across words. For instance, as mentioned earlier, it has been demonstrated that vowel nasality is a strong perceptual cue to the nasal-oral status of the following consonant (Ali et al., 1971; Beddor et al., 2013; Lahiri & Marslen-Wilson, 1991; Warren & Marslen-Wilson, 1987). There is also evidence that listeners are sensitive to variations in the strength of the cue: CVN words are recognized faster when the prenasal vowels occur with stronger cues for nasality than when these cues are weaker (Beddor et al., 2013; Scarborough & Zellou, 2013; Zellou & Dahan, 2019). These cues can be maintained in memory, as demonstrated by studies showing that people's own articulation of nasal-final words is influenced by the degree of nasality of the talker they are exposed to and who they unconsciously imitate (Zellou et al., 2017).

1.3 Individual Differences in Phonological Grammars for Coarticulation

Phonological models that assume linguistic categories are formed from remembered tokens (Pierrehumbert, 2002) also presuppose that each speaker will have unique linguistic representations, since every individual has distinct perceptual experiences. Indeed, there is much prior work suggesting that individuals within a speech community might vary in their phonological grammars for coarticulation (Beddor, 2009; Yu & Zellou, 2019; Zellou, 2017). Examining individual variation in coarticulatory vowel nasalization can also inform models of sound change. In particular, inherent in both the Ohala (1993) and Beddor (2009) models of coarticulatory variation as a pathway to sound change is the idea that reanalysis of nasal coarticulation as an intended, deliberate feature of the vowel is a process that happens in an individual during spoken word comprehension. For instance, Ohala's hypocorrection model frames the mini sound change event as happening in real time, in an interaction between a speaker and a hearer. Thus, the idea that an individual might phonologize coarticulatory nasalization as a pathway toward sound change on a community level is consistent with the most widely accepted models of sound change.

Beddor (2009) reports individual differences in perceptual sensitivity for coarticulatory vowel nasalization: Based on their performance on a paired discrimination task, where their perceptual sensitivity to coarticulatory vowel nasalization was assessed, Beddor categorized listeners into two groups. One group of listeners displayed sensitivity to the total duration of nasality present across the vowel and the consonant, even as its temporal alignment varied across stimuli; these individuals were classified as "perceptual equivalence" listeners, since they treated equally sized velum-lowering gestures as similar even if their temporal alignment over the syllable rhyme varied. Another group displayed sensitivity to the extent of nasalization present on the vowel alone; these individuals were classified as "vowel nasalization" listeners since they attended to the temporal extent of vowel nasality only, regardless of the nasal consonant duration. These distinct perceptual strategies might be indicative of distinct phonological grammars of coarticulatory vowel nasalization.

Zellou (2017) explored differences in the relationship between individuals' production and perception of nasal coarticulation within a speech community. Using perceptual methods similar to those in Beddor and Krakow (1999), she observed variation across individuals' patterns of partial perceptual compensation, which in turn was linked to their own produced patterns of nasal coarticulation. Individuals who produced less extensive nasal coarticulation exhibited more partial compensation, while individuals who produced more extensive nasal coarticulation were more likely to compensate fully for vowel nasalization in the context of a nasal consonant. Put another way, those who produced more extensive coarticulation showed greater perceptual use of coarticulation in identifying the nasal coda than those who produced less coarticulation. The results of this study suggest a strong connection between an individual's prior idiosyncratic experience, reflected in their representations used to produce speech, and those used during perceptual compensation.

Taken together, findings suggest that individuals can have unique coarticulatory grammars in perception (Beddor, 2009) and the perception-production link (Zellou, 2017). What would individual differences in phonologization of coarticulatory vowel nasalization look like? Zellou (2017) proposed that individuals who produce greater degrees of coarticulatory vowel nasalization have phonologized vowel nasality more than those who produce less. Yet, her finding that those who produce more coarticulation display *more* perceptual compensation for coarticulation than those who produce less coarticulatory nasalization is not consistent with that interpretation. Specifically, Beddor's (2009) classification of listeners as displaying perceptual sensitivity either to the duration of nasalization over the syllable rhyme (perceptual equivalence-listeners) or just over the vowel duration (vowel nasalization-listeners) is reminiscent of Solé's (2007) cross-language production-based typology of speakers whose coarticulatory extent covaries with nasal coda duration (Spanish) and speakers who target vowel nasalization as an inherent feature of the vowel (English) (this study will be reviewed in greater detail in Section 2). Can we find individual variation in these production patterns, reflecting differences in the grammatical status of coarticulation for speakers, *within a speech community*?

Comparing phonetic patterns across languages has been an effective way to identify what aspects of speech are grammatically specified or not. As outlined, there is much prior work establishing language-specific coarticulatory patterns, above and beyond what can be explained by motoric principles in many cases, leading to the well-established understanding that nasal coarticulatory patterns, for example, are represented in the grammar of speakers. We propose that such an approach can be an effective way at examining cross-speaker variation within a language.

1.4 Current Study

The current Element is focused on further understanding how nasal-coarticulatory detail is represented by the cognitive system and, ultimately, how distinct phonetic and phonological patterns develop over time and are used functionally in linguistic communication. In a set of studies, we explore further the hypothesis that individuals within a language can have distinct grammars for coarticulation, in particular building on prior frameworks that have identified differences in grammaticalized versus mechanical coarticulatory processes. The experiments presented in this Element were designed to examine individual differences in speakers' realization of coarticulatory nasality in the oral-nasal phonological contrast in American English. Solé (1992, 1995, 2007) proposed a diagnostic for identifying across languages whether coarticulatory patterns are grammatically specified or biomechanical. Since coarticulation is gestural overlap, she proposed that biomechanically constrained coarticulatory extent would covary with temporal-prosodic reorganization of utterances since changes to global articulation rate would affect the gestural implementation of sounds. Meanwhile, grammatically specified phonetic patterns are targeted by speakers as a meaningful property of the speech signal. Thus, deliberate coarticulation would be produced consistently across speaking tempos. Using these criteria, she compared acoustic patterns of vowels in CVVN words produced by native Continental Spanish and native American English speakers at different speaking rates. English speakers produced the same degree of coarticulatory vowel nasalization as the absolute duration segments vary due to changes in speaking rates across utterances; thus, English was categorized as having grammatically specified vowel nasalization in words with a nasal coda (i.e., /ṼN/). In contrast, as Spanish speakers' vowel duration increased due to speaking rate, degree of coarticulation decreased; this was taken to indicate that gestural overlap was a mechanical feature of articulation and not a linguistically specified feature (i.e., /VN/ in Spanish). This was taken as evidence of differences in the grammatical specification in coarticulation across the two languages. In Experiment 1, we use this as a framework for typologizing different realizations of coarticulatory nasalization across languages to differences in the realization of coarticulation across sixty speakers of American English as grammaticalized or not based on production patterns. Theoretical work has argued that individuals within a speech community can vary in the phonologization of coarticulation as a grammatical-specified, inherent aspect of lexical items (Yu & Zellou, 2019). Thus, we extend Solé's method for classifying languages as having phonologized or phonetic coarticulatory patterns by applying it to categorize individuals within a language into these categories.

We also explore cross-speaker variations in coarticulatory patterns from a perceptual perspective. As reviewed earlier in this section, there is evidence that listeners are highly sensitive to within-category variations of nasal coarticulatory patterns in encoding lexical contrasts (Beddor et al., 2013; Zellou & Dahan, 2019). Moreover, listener-based models of sound change posit that mechanisms of diachronic variation are perceptually oriented (e.g., Ohala, 1993). Thus, Experiment 2 aims to *perceptually define* cross-speaker variation in coarticulatory vowel nasalization, exploring the implications of cross-speaker coarticulatory variations for listener-based phonological categorizations. In Experiment 2, truncated CV syllables (i.e., CVC and CVN words with the coda spliced out) from the sixty speakers from Experiment 1 were presented to listeners who performed word-completion decisions on each item. This perceptual paradigm has been used in prior work in order to investigate the representation of nasalization on lexical items across languages. For instance, Lahiri and Marlsen-Wilson (1991) used this methodology to compare the phonological status of vowel nasalization for English and Hindi listeners. They found that English listeners were unlikely to identify a CṼ truncated syllable as originating from a CVN word, which they argued was evidence for underspecification of coarticulatory nasalization in the lexicon of English. Yet, Ohala and Ohala (1995) performed a replication of the Lahiri and Marslen-Wilson (1991) study, finding evidence to support the opposite conclusion – that English listeners do encode coarticulatory details on words and use them to identify lexical items. In the current study, we use this methodology as a way to probe cross-speaker differences in the phonologization of coarticulatory vowel nasalization within American English, as either having phonologized coarticulatory nasalization, in which we predict that listeners will be very accurate at identifying those speakers' truncated CṼ syllables as CVN words, or not.

Finally, we relate the production and perceptual assessments as a way to comprehensively categorize variation across speakers in the phonologization of coarticulatory nasalization.

2 Experiment 1: Quantifying Individual Differences in Phonologization in Production

A series of seminal studies by Solé (1992, 1995, 2007) lays out a framework for investigating how the relationship between anticipatory nasal coarticulation and temporal organization of segments can be used to determine whether coarticulatory patterns are purely the result of phonetic implementation or phonologized. Solé's work compares production of CVVN utterances in American English and Continental Spanish. She proposes that coarticulatory patterns that are linguistically specified, that is, phonologized, should covary with durational variation so that changes in temporal organization of segments (due to speaking rate, for instance) should not change the relative coarticulatory patterns. In other words, targeted and deliberate coarticulation should occur to the same extent regardless of the absolute duration of the vowel. This was observed in the speech of American English speakers, where their productions displayed a one-to-one relationship between the duration of the vowel and the duration of vowel nasalization. This was interpreted as reflecting phonologized coarticulatory nasality because speakers displayed active maintenance of nasalization on the vowel: as speakers sped up or slowed down their speech rate, degree of nasalization varied in tandem with changes in vowel duration.

In contrast, the Spanish speakers' productions of these words displayed a constant duration of vowel nasalization as their speech rate varied: as vowel length lengthened or shortened with speaking rate, the constant duration of the overlapping velum gesture led to less or more coarticulation, respectively. Solé (2007) argued that the velum-lowering gesture was timed relative to the coda consonant in Spanish, thus it was not a linguistically relevant feature of the vowel. Hence, nasal coarticulation in Spanish is classified as biomechanically specified. Figure 1 schematizes the different categorizations of coarticulation repertoires that might exist across speakers. Figure 1 A.i depicts a speaker whose coarticulatory patterns are deliberate (here, we use the term "phonological" as a categorization since such a speaker would be producing deliberate, controlled anticipatory coarticulation patterns); following her own criteria, Solé identified that English is classified as a language with this anticipatory nasal coarticulation pattern. As the temporal patterns of the nasal coda and the vowel

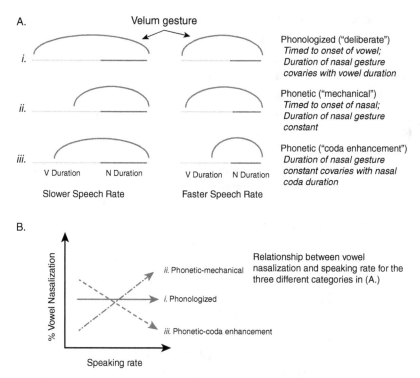

Figure 1 Schematic of the types of relationships between temporal patterns and degree of coarticulatory vowel nasality.

vary, the velum gesture is targeted to synchronize with the onset of the vowel. In slower or faster speaking rates, the amount of overlap of the velum gesture on the vowel remains stable. In other words, while the temporal relationship between the nasal consonant and the vowel varies across utterances, the speaker maintains constant vowel nasalization on the vowel. This would be realized as a flat relationship between vowel nasalization and speech rate, as illustrated in Figure 1 B.i. Since the timing of the onset of anticipatory coarticulation is maintained regardless of the temporal reorganization of segments, this speaker can be categorized as having phonologized vowel nasalization. In other words, for this speaker, vowel nasalization is a linguistically specified property, even in the context of a nasal coda.

Figure 1 A.ii depicts a speaker whose coarticulatory patterns can be described as "mechanical." For this speaker, the velum-lowering gesture is timed in relation to the nasal coda, and its overlap with the preceding vowel is physiological in nature. As prosodic organization varies for this speaker, the magnitude of the temporal extent of coarticulatory nasalization remains constant. This will be realized as less coarticulatory nasalization in slower speaking rates, but increased coarticulation in faster speaking rates since the vowel duration varies but duration of the velum gesture overlapping with the vowel does not. In Figure 1 B.ii, this is reflected as a positive relationship between proportion of vowel nasalization and speaking rate. This type of speaker can be classified as having phonetic, nongrammatical implementation because their coarticulatory features are scaled up or scaled down depending on rate, thus can be attributed to a biomechanical origin. Solé demonstrated that Spanish speakers, on average, display this pattern.

Solé's (2007) conceptualization of a "mechanical" coarticulator is that this type of pattern is not under the speaker's control. However, other models of phonetic variation that relate extent of coarticulatory variation and durational properties of utterances take the stance that such a relationship is targeted by speakers. For instance, Lindblom's (1990) characterization of coarticulation in the H&H model is consistent with Solé's proposal for Spanish. Lindblom also sees the default "low cost" form of behavior by the motor system is increased coarticulation since it facilitates production of adjacent distinct articulations, thus he predicts it will be increased under "hypospeech" (i.e., faster speech conditions). In fact, there is evidence that some English speakers might adopt this approach, as well. Studies by Cho, Kim, and Kim (2017) and Jang, Kim, and Cho (2018) have investigated how coarticulatory vowel nasalization varies as a function of prosodic structure in English (and Korean). They find that vowels in CVN words produced in prosodically strong and prominent positions (either being phrase-initial or under contrastive focus) are produced with less coarticulatory nasalization than those in weaker positions. These effects are considered to be not low-level mechanical effects, but rather are interpreted as under speaker control and deliberate. Specifically, Cho and colleagues argue that, consistent with the concept of "localized hyperarticulation" (de Jong, 1995, 2004), reduction of coarticulation in CVN words in slower speech rates is a targeting and enhancement of the [oral] feature of vowels. For instance, rather than regressive nasal consonant to vowel coarticulation, hyperarticulation can also be realized as progressive oral-vowel to nasal consonant coarticulation. A related type of variation in the timing of nasalization has been observed on partially nasalized consonants; for instance, Wetzels and Nevins (2018) report on cases where partially nasalized stops (e.g., $[m^{b}a]$) might have arisen diachronically from situations where the orality of the adjacent vowel is enhanced and overlaps on a nasal segment, leading to a partially nasalized allophone as observed in languages such as Kaingang (Southern Jê, Brazil) and Negarotê (Northern Nambikwara).

Meanwhile, in consideration of Beddor's (2009) proposal that speaker-specific grammars for vowels in CVN contexts can vary, we might also predict a third type of speaker classification: those who aim to *enhance the nasality of the coda* under more careful (i.e., slower) speaking conditions. Beddor (2009) posits that coarticulation is perceptually informative, in that it is something that speakers use in a highly controlled manner to provide early and redundant information about the underlying segments. For instance, enhanced coarticulation on a prenasal vowel can help the listener determine just by hearing [bĩ] that the word is "bean" not "bead" (Beddor et al., 2013; Zellou & Dahan, 2019). Work done by Scarborough and colleagues (e.g., Scarborough, 2012, 2013; Scarborough & Zellou, 2013; Zellou & Scarborough, 2019) explores how nasal coarticulatory production patterns might be perceptually oriented to enhance lexical distinctiveness. In contexts where there is an ostensible pressure to make speech more intelligible (e.g., for words that are more confusable due to a large number of phonological neighbors and in communicative tasks with an interlocutor where there is an authentic pressure to be more intelligible), Scarborough and colleagues have found that speakers produce a greater extent of nasal coarticulation than in situations with less output-oriented pressure. This is also found *in tandem with* increases in temporal properties. For instance, more highly confusable words spoken to real listeners are produced with both longer vowel duration and greater extent of coarticulatory nasalization than less confusable words (Scarborough & Zellou, 2013). In that same study, those items, as well as others produced in a condition that did not elicit coarticulatory enhancement, were used as stimuli in a lexical decision task. Scarborough et al. found that the more confusable words were easier for listeners to identify when they contained enhanced coarticulatory features than those that did not. There is also cross-linguistic evidence for such a strategy. Avelino et al. (2020) report that in Kakataibo (a Panoan language of Peru) words with nasal consonants contain increased coarticulatory vowel nasalization when stressed. The authors argue that this serves a functional purpose by making the cues to the phonological category of the adjacent nasal consonants more perceptually salient on the vowels.

Hence, the strategy of increasing coarticulatory vowel nasality in slower speech conditions as a listener-oriented speech style is another potential speaker behavior. This third possible type of speaker is schematized in Figure 1 A.iii. Here, coarticulatory patterns also vary in tandem with temporal factors, but in the reverse direction of Figure 1 A.ii: as speaking rate decreases, temporal extent of nasal coarticulation on the vowel increases. This scenario depicts a speaker in conditions that both lead to slower speaking rate and to an enhancement of the coarticulatory features resulting from the consonant. In this case, enhancement of the nasal coda could lead to enhancement of the [+nasal] feature of that segment, resulting in larger coarticulatory extent on preceding vowels. Such a speaker is theoretically possible under the view that certain speakers might slow speaking rate to make segments more intelligible to interlocutors and enhancement of the cues that help listeners anticipate upcoming segments is part of this goal. Thus, slower speech rates might contain greater coarticulatory cues, consistent with what has been reported in prior studies, namely that more hyperarticulated speech conditions, and those that are more perceptually beneficial for listeners, contained both longer segments and greater degrees of coarticulatory nasalization (Scarborough & Zellou, 2013; Zellou & Scarborough, 2015).

In Experiment 1, we will use these three distinct speech rate–coarticulation relationships as hypothetical heuristics for investigating cross-speaker variation in American English.

2.1 Methods

2.1.1 Participants

Sixty University of California–Davis (UC Davis) undergraduates participated in this study (forty-nine female, eleven male; age range = 18–33 years old; average age = 19.6 years old), recruited through the UC Davis psychology subject pool. All were native speakers of American English and most reported living in California for the majority of their lives (out of the sixty speakers, only one reported living in California for 6 months, one for 1.5 years, and one for 6 years; all others reported 12+ years living in California). They all received course credit for their participation. None reported any visual or hearing impairment.

2.1.2 Materials and Procedure

The target words consisted of five sets of CVC-CVN-NVN minimal triplets containing non-high vowels (/ɑ/, /æ/, /ʌ/, /ɛ/, /ow/): *bod, bon, non; bad, ban, nam; bud, bun, numb; bed, ben, men; bode, bone, known.* Participants produced each word twice in the carrier phrase "__ the word is __." Each target word utterance was repeated twice. Sixty-two filler words were also included in the list that participants produced. The utterances were presented in random order to participants, who read each utterance out loud (in some rare cases, a participant repeated an utterance on a given trial if they made a speech error; correct productions of target words in repeated utterances in these cases were included in the analysis). The target words were extracted from the carrier phrases.

The experiment was conducted over a single 30-minute session in a soundproof booth at the UC Davis Phonetics Lab. Auditory recordings were made using a Shure WH20 XLR head-mounted microphone and digitally sampled at a 44-kHz rate.

2.1.3 Acoustic Measurements

Vowels were segmented automatically, using FAVE force-alignment (Rosenfelder et al., 2011), in the utterances produced by participants. Vowel segmentations were hand-corrected in the target words using the following segmentation criteria: the onset and offset of the vowels were taken to be the points at which an abrupt increase or decrease in amplitude of the higher-formant frequencies was observed in the spectrogram. An abrupt change in amplitude in the waveform, along with simplification of waveform cycles, was used to verify these segmentations. Two types of acoustic measurements were obtained from each of the isolated vowels from each of the participants.

First, speech rate (number of syllables per second) was measured over each sentence (e.g., "ban, the word is ban") using a Praat script (De Jong et al., 2017). While speaking rate was not manipulated in any explicit way during the speech-production elicitation, speaking rate varied naturally over sentences within speakers (average per-speaker minimum speaking rate = 1.1 syll/s; average per-speaker maximum speaking rate = 2.9 syll/s).

Next, acoustic vowel nasalization was measured acoustically using A1-P0, a measure derived from spectral characteristics of vowel nasalization (Chen, 1997). Nasalized vowels show the presence of an extra low-frequency spectral peak (P0), generally below the first formant, accompanied by a concomitant reduction in the amplitude of the first formant spectral peak (A1). The acoustic manifestation of vowel nasalization may be quantified, then, by examining the relative amplitudes of the nasal peak (in non-high vowels, where F1 and P0 would be separate) and the first formant in a measure A1-P0. Since P0 increases and A1 decreases as nasalization increases, a smaller A1-P0 difference indicates greater acoustic nasality. Measurements of A1-P0 were made on the segmented vowels, at the eight equidistant points of each vowel automatically, using a Praat script, and hand-verified.

2.1.4 Normalization of Acoustic Nasality: Degree of Vowel Nasalization

Raw A1-P0 values vary widely across speakers (e.g., Chen, 1997; Styler, 2017). In order to have a reliable across-speaker measure for relative degree of nasalization, A1-P0 values can be normalized relative to the minimum and maximum values (in NVN and CVC contexts, respectively) (Jang et al., 2018;

Zellou, 2017). Using this method, the A1-P0 values from each speaker's CVC, CVN, and NVN words are used to assess how much anticipatory coarticulation is present on each vowel relative to their overall minimum and maximum produced nasality (i.e., difference in A1-P0 for CVC and NVN contexts). Hence, for each observation, a normalized coarticulation measurement was assessed by dividing the difference in nasality produced in the speaker's most oral CVC (max A1-P0) and the observation ($\text{A1-P0}_{\text{CVC Max a1p0}} - \text{A1-P0}_{\text{observed}}$) by the total range in A1-P0 observed in all CVC and NVN words. Since the difference between CVC and NVN captures the maximal degree of nasality produced ($\text{A1-P0}_{\text{CVC Max a1-p0}} - \text{A1-P0}_{\text{NVN Min a1-p0}}$), the resulting measurement is a proportional score, for each observation, representing the ratio of produced vowel nasality divided by total produced nasality range, where values lie between 0 and 1. A larger coarticulation proportion value indicates that the observation contains nasality values closer to that speaker's maximum level of nasalization in NVN words, whereas a smaller coarticulation proportion value indicates that the observation contains nasality closer to the least nasal (most oral) CVC vowel. The formula for this normalized nasality calculation is provided in Equation (1).

$$\left(\text{A1-P0}_{\text{CVC MAX A1-P0}} - \text{A1-P0}_{\text{Observed}}\right) / \left(\text{A1-P0}_{\text{CVC MAX A1-P0}}\right.$$
$$\left. - \text{A1-P0}_{\text{NVN MIN A1-P0}}\right) \qquad (1)$$

This normalized vowel nasalization proportion score was computed for each data point.

2.2 Results

Figure 2 displays mean vowel nasalization values across the eight equidistant vowel timepoints for all sixty speakers' productions of CVC, CVN, and NVN sets. As seen, values for speakers' NVN words are both overall largest, indicating the greatest amount of vowel nasalization, and flattest throughout the portion of the vowel duration. This is consistent with a stable velum-lowering gesture that starts before the vowel onset (for the onset nasal consonant) and continues throughout the entire production of the vowel (Cohn, 1990). Vowel nasalization values are smallest for vowels in CVC items, consistent with these vowels not being coarticulated with nasal consonants. However, there is a slight increase in degree of vowel nasalization in CVC vowels over the duration of the vowel. It has also been observed in prior work that oral vowels can sometimes be produced with a small amount of vowel nasalization; under the view that these vowels are underspecified for nasalization, the presence of a slight amount of nasality has been reported in prior work (e.g., Solé, 2007). Finally, it can be seen that the amount of vowel nasalization on vowels in CVN contexts is the

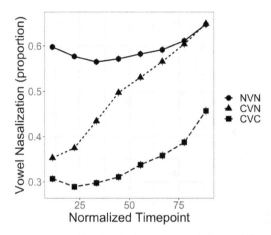

Figure 2 Mean vowel nasalization values across eight equidistant timepoints aggregated across sixty speakers' productions of CVC, CVN, and NVN words. Bars depict standard errors of the mean.

most dynamic over the production of the vowel. Vowels in CVN contexts start with a very small amount of nasalization, close to the amount observed in CVC vowels, but degree of vowel nasalization increases steadily over time. At later portions of vowels in CVN items, degree of nasalization is comparable to that observed in vowels in NVN contexts.

Figure 3 provides averaged vowel nasalization values for each of the sixty speakers' CVC (squares), CVN (triangles), and NVN (circles) items. As seen, there is a great deal of variation across speakers in their patterns of vowel nasalization, particularly in the relationship between vowel nasalization on vowels in CVN items and those in oral and fully nasalized vowels. Some speakers exhibit degrees of nasalization in CVN items very similar to those produced in their NVN vowels (such as S129 at the far right side of Figure 3), while some speakers exhibit nasalization in CVN comparable to that in CVC items (such as S088 in the middle of Figure 3).

Vowel nasalization values across the eight timepoints for vowels in CVC and CVN contexts were analyzed using a mixed effects linear regression model using the *lmer()* function in the *lme4* package (Bates et al., 2016). Estimates for degrees of freedom, *t*-statistics, and *p*-values were computed using Satterthwaite approximation with the *lmerTest* package (Kuznetsova et al., 2017). The model included fixed effects of Structure (CVN vs. CVC), Speech Rate (syllables/sec), vowel Timepoint, the interaction between Structure and Speech Rate, and the interaction between Structure and Timepoint. The model included the maximal random effects structure with by-participant random intercepts and by-participant random slopes for all main effects and each interaction.

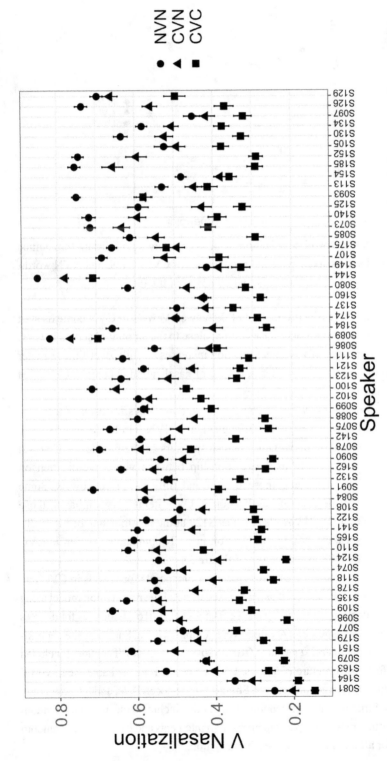

Figure 3 Mean vowel nasalization values for CVC, CVN, and NVN words for each of the sixty speakers (values averaged across eight equidistant timepoints). Speakers are ordered from having the overall lowest average degree of vowel nasalization to the highest. Bars depict standard errors of the mean.

In addition to using the mixed effects model to characterize population-level production patterns, this model was also used to test hypotheses about individual differences in vowel nasalization as a function of phonological structure, timepoint, and speaking rate changes. These person-specific, adjusted residual slopes were extracted from the model using the *ranef()* function.

The summary statistics for the fixed effects of the model are provided in Table 1. The model computed a significant main effect of Timepoint wherein degree of vowel nasalization increases over the duration of the vowel, on average. There was also a significant interaction between Structure and Timepoint. This was seen in Figure 2: over time, vowels in CVN contexts become much more nasalized than vowels in CVC contexts. Speaking Rate did not participate in any significant main effects or interactions. This is consistent with prior work by Solé (1995, 2007) which found that, in English, as speaking rate changes, degree of vowel nasalization remains constant (equivalent degree of vowel nasalization regardless of changes in speech rate). The lack of a significant interaction between Structure and Speaking Rate suggests that, on aggregate, this observation holds for these data.

However, as seen in Figure 4, which displays random effects of the model, there is considerable variation across speakers in patterns of vowel nasalization as a function of context and speaking rate. The right two panels of Figure 4 provide the residual, individual vowel nasalization slope terms for Structure (bottom far right) and the interaction between Structure and Speaking Rate (top far right). As seen, there is considerable deviation across individuals in vowel nasalization difference between CVC and CVN vowels (bottom far right) and in

Table 1 Summary statistics of the fixed effects of the model run on Vowel Nasalization values.
Equation: *lmer(VowelNasalization~Timepoint*Structure+Speechrate*Structure (1+Timepoint*Structure+Speechrate*Structure|Speaker).*

	Estimate	Std. error	df	t	p
(Intercept)	0.257	0.023	54.27	11.04	<0.001
Timepoint	0.021	0.002	58.72	9.98	<0.001
Structure: CVN (vs. CVC)	0.039	0.024	43.31	1.61	0.115
Speaking Rate	−0.015	0.008	51.17	−1.74	0.088
Timepoint * Structure	0.023	0.002	59.46	13.68	<0.001
Structure * Speaking Rate	−0.002	0.010	46.69	−0.15	0.879

Speaker

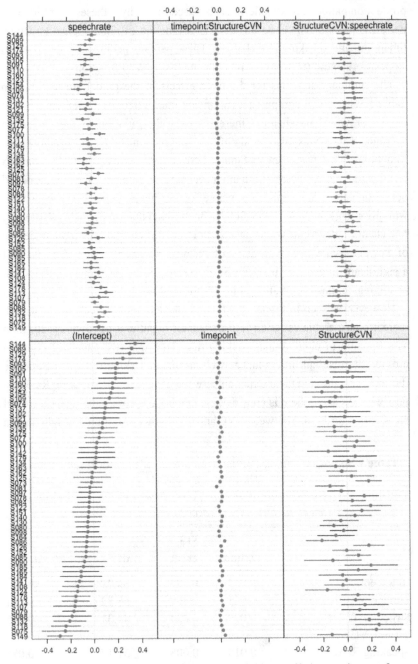

Figure 4 Each panel shows the speaker-specific coefficient estimates for different effects, as extracted from the model reported in Table 1.

an individual's slope for vowel nasalization in CVN words as a function of Speaking Rate (top far right).

The deviations across speakers' coefficients observed in Figure 4 reflect the variety of different acoustic patterns used to realize the oral-nasalized vowel contrast. For instance, there is variation both in positive and negative directions for the slope terms for both the interactions. With respect to speech rate, the coefficients in the top far right panel reflect speaker-specific residual slopes for the influence of speaking rate on degree of vowel nasalization in vowels in CVN contexts. A coefficient for this effect equal to or close to 0 reflects an individual whose degree of vowel nasalization does not vary with changes in speaking rate. Such an individual can be categorized as a "controlled" coarticulatory nasality speaker, following the classifications made by Solé (2007): these speakers produce a constant level of nasality that is timed with respect to the vowel onset rather than the start of the nasal coda which will vary with speech rate. Solé (2007) actually classifies English as having a controlled coarticulatory implementation, following this assessment. Furthermore, Solé uses this metric to conclude that coarticulatory nasality is phonologized in English, yet does not look for variation across speakers within English.

Meanwhile, following Solé's framework, a positive coefficient for this term can signal a speaker with a "mechanical" coarticulatory repertoire: as speaking rate increases, there is a constant duration of an overlapping velum gesture since nasalization is timed with the onset of the nasal coda consonant; thus, degree of nasality on the vowel will increase or decrease with rate. Thus, speakers with a positive coefficient for the slope of speech rate for CVN vowels can be classified as having phonetic (i.e., nonphonologized) coarticulatory patterns. Note that several speakers do indeed have positive coefficients for this effect.

Finally, several speakers also display *negative* coefficient values for the effect of speaking rate on vowel nasalization. Variation with speaking rate is consistent with a phonetic classification in Solé's framework. However, a negative coefficient implies that as these speakers' speech rate decreases, degree of vowel nasalization increases (and vice versa). Such a pattern is consistent with work by Cho and colleagues examining phonetic *enhancement* of the phonological feature [+nasal] in the nasal consonant (Cho et al., 2017; Jang et al., 2018). Specifically, they have shown that in both Korean and English, under conditions of prosodic focus, nasal codas lengthen and exert a stronger coarticulatory effect on the preceding vowel. Indeed, our frame sentences could have been interpreted as prompting prosodic focus on the lexical items ("ban, the word is ban"), leading some speakers to adopt that strategy. This enhancement strategy can also be classified as a "mechanical," i.e., nonphonologized, coarticulatory pattern since these speakers exhibit variations in degree of coarticulation with changes in prosodic structure that can be explained via articulatory timing relationships between the nasal coda and the velum.

There is also a large amount of variation across speaker coefficients in the effect associated with CVN Structure. Again, coefficients for speakers can be both positive, indicating above-average difference in degree of vowel nasalization between CVC and CVN vowels (a speaker with a great amount of coarticulatory vowel nasalization), and negative, indicating below-average oral-nasal vowel difference (a speaker with a smaller amount of nasal coarticulation).

In order to characterize more precisely how speakers vary in the relationship between speaking rate and degree of nasalization, a second model was run only on vowel nasalization vowels in CVN words at an early timepoint in the vowel (at ~12 percent of vowel duration). At this early timepoint, changes in degree of vowel nasalization as a function of speaking rate will be more extreme. Thus, we can better characterize whether vowel nasalization patterns are constant across speaking rates (controlled) or temporally determined (through mechanical or enhancement mechanisms). The model consisted of a fixed effect of Speaking Rate (syllables/seconds), random intercepts for speaker, and by-speaker random slopes for speaking rate. Similar to the previously mentioned Timepoint model, there was not a significant coefficient associated with speaking rate [$Est = -0.005$, SE $= 0.01$, $t = -0.45$, $p = 0.65$], again supporting the interpretation that, on average, at this early vowel timepoint, American English speakers do not display changes in degree of nasalization in tandem with changes in speaking rate.

However, inspection of the speaker-specific random slopes for speaking rate reveals a great deal of variation across individuals. The speaker-specific slopes extracted from this model were extracted using *ranef()* and then used to categorize speakers in how changes in speech rate can be related to changes in degree of vowel nasalization. Individuals with a slope value close to zero (>-0.01, <0.01) were categorized as "phonologized" speakers, since changes in speaking rate cannot be related to variations in degree of nasalization across productions of CVN words. (These numeric cut-offs are somewhat arbitrary, but rather rigid). Speakers with a positive slope value (>0.01) were classified as "mechanical" coarticulators, since changes in speaking rate are positively correlated with changes in coarticulatory vowel nasalization. Those with a negative slope value (<-0.01) were classified as "enhancers," following the reasoning that if slower speech rate led to increases in degree of coarticulation then those individuals are providing greater coarticulatory information when they are producing more careful speech. Figure 5 shows the relationship between speaking rate (syllables per second) and degree of vowel nasalization

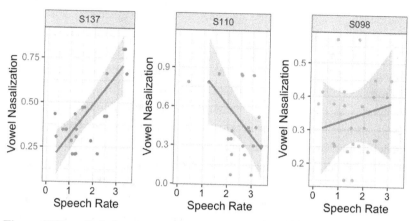

Figure 5 Plots depicting the relationship between speaking rate and degree of vowel nasalization for three speakers who exemplify the distinct categories of coarticulators, based on slopes extracted from a random effects model run on vowel nasalization from an early timepoint of CVN productions. S137 is categorized as a "mechanical" coarticulator who displays a positive relationship between speaking rate and degree of coarticulatory nasalization present early in the vowel; S110 exemplifies an "enhancement" coarticulation strategy, a negative relationship; S098 reflects a "phonologized" coarticulation, wherein degree of vowel nasalization is not related to changes in speaking rate.

in an early timepoint (~12 percent of vowel duration) for vowels produced in CVN items by three different types of speaker following these categorizations.

Using the criteria of categorizing individuals based on their speaker-specific slopes, twenty-three (out of sixty) speakers were classified as having "phonologized" coarticulatory patterns, sixteen speakers were classified as being "mechanical" coarticulators, and twenty-one were classified as being coarticulatory "enhancers." Figure 5 shows the relationship between speaking rate and degree of vowel nasalization in the earliest vowel timepoint for CVN words averaged within each of these categories. As seen, on average, speakers in the mechanical, enhancement, and phonologized categories display distinct relationships between degree of coarticulatory nasalization and speaking rate, as predicted in the schematic in Figure 1. On average, Mechanical coarticulators have low degree of vowel nasalization at early timepoints when the speaking rate is very slow, yet as speaking rate increases, vowel nasalization increases. In contrast, Enhancers have a high degree of coarticulatory nasalization early in the vowel when speaking rate is very slow, but they *decrease* degree of nasalization as speaking rate increases. Meanwhile, those with phonologized

coarticulatory patterns display the same amount of coarticulatory vowel nasalization at all speaking rates.

An additional mixed effect linear regression was run on these data to
confirm the difference across groups. The model was fit to the vowel nasalization values at the early timepoint in CVN words. A fixed effect of Speaker
Category was included in the model (three levels: phonologized [reference
level], mechanical, enhancement). Speaking Rate was also included in the
model, along with an interaction between Speaker Category and Speaking
Rate. The model also included by-speaker random intercepts and by-speaker
random slopes for Speaking Rate. The model output is provided in Table 2.
First, Speaker Category had a significant effect on degree of vowel nasalization at the early vowel timepoint. Relative to phonologized coarticulators,
Mechanical coarticulators produced *less* coarticulatory vowel nasalization.
This is consistent with the categorizations of these speakers as "phonologized" and "mechanical": those who display phonological patterns of coarticulatory nasalization should also produce it to a greater magnitude than those
whose realization of coarticulation is biomechanical in origin. The coefficient
associated with Enhancers was positive and also significant. This suggests
that Enhancers produce *even greater* coarticulatory vowel nasalization than

Table 2 Summary statistics of the fixed effects of the model run on Vowel
Nasalization values in CVN words at the earliest vowel timepoint.
Equation: *lmer(VowelNasalization~SpeakerCategory*Speech Rate
(1+Speech Rate|Speaker).*

	Estimate	**Std. error**	**df**	***t***	***p***
(Intercept)	0.34	0.04	212.36	9.31	<0.001
Speaker Category: Mechanical (vs. Phonologized)	−0.19	0.05	163.62	−3.85	<0.001
Speaker Category: Enhancement (vs. Phonologized)	0.24	0.05	171.20	4.98	<0.001
Speaking rate	0.00	0.02	350.35	−0.01	0.99
Speaker Category: Mechanical * Speaking Rate	0.07	0.02	260.57	3.14	<0.001
Speaker Category: Enhancement * Speaking Rate	−0.07	0.02	292.22	−3.30	<0.001

those who display "phonologized" vowel nasality. This is also in line with the idea that enhancers are actively controlling the degree of vowel nasalization and do so to enhance the phonological features of the upcoming coda consonant.

Speaking rate was not a significant main effect, consistent with the prior statistical models run on these data. However, there were significant interactions between speaking rate and speaker category. First, there was a significant positive coefficient associated with the interaction between speaking rate and Mechanical coarticulators, relative to the reference level (Phonologized). Second, there was a significant negative slope for the interaction between speaking rate and Enhancing coarticulators. These significant interactions confirm the relationships between speaking rate and degree of coarticulation across the three groups observed in Figure 6.

Finally, having established that these three speaker categories can be classified as having distinct relationships between speaking rate and degree of vowel nasalization at the earliest vowel timepoint, we also explored whether these speaker types were distinct in other relevant acoustic-phonetic properties. For instance, perhaps "enhancers" just produce longer, slower vowels overall. Or, maybe speaker categories differ in overall degree of vowel nasalization produced. To investigate these questions, we ran two separate linear mixed effects

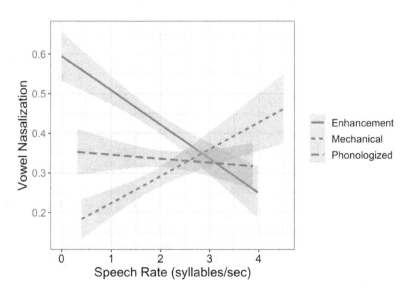

Figure 6 Regression lines fitted to data from the earliest timepoint of vowels in CVN words, for speakers categorized as having "enhancement," "mechanical," or "phonologized" coarticulatory vowel nasalization based on extracted speaker-specific slopes.

models on these acoustic features in CVN words: one on vowel duration and one on vowel nasalization at midpoint. Both models had identical structure, containing a main fixed predictor of Speaker Category (Phonologized [reference level], Mechanical, Enhancer) and random intercepts for each Speaker.

The vowel duration model did not reveal a main effect of speaker category: relative to "phonologized" speakers (mean vowel duration = 223.5 msec), mechanical speakers did not differ in vowel duration (223.2 msec) [$Coef = -0.26$, $SE = 9.3$, $t = -0.03$, $p = 0.97$]. Enhancer speakers (mean vowel duration = 224.9 msec) also did not produce different vowel durations from phonologized speakers [$Coef = 1.24$, $SE = 8.6$, $t = 0.14$, $p = 0.88$].

The vowel nasalization model revealed no difference in produced coarticulatory vowel nasalization between "phonologized" (midpoint mean = 48 percent vowel nasalization) and "mechanical" speakers (midpoint mean = 44 percent vowel nasalization) [$Coef = -0.05$, $SE = 0.03$, $t = -1.38$, $p = 0.17$]. However, "enhancers" did produce significantly larger vowel nasalization (midpoint mean = 55 percent vowel nasalization [$Coef = 0.07$, $SE = 0.03$, $t = 2.2$, $p < 0.05$].

2.3 Experiment 1 Interim Discussion

Prior work has investigated the relationship between anticipatory coarticulatory patterns in production as a function of prosodic-temporal organization (Cho et al., 2017; Solé, 1992, 1995, 2007). This relationship has been shown to vary across languages and has been used as way of typologizing the grammatical status of nasal coarticulation as either mechanical (i.e., purely physiological in origin, therefore not specified in the grammar) or deliberate (i.e., a linguistically specified and targeted property of the vowel and thus phonologized) (Solé, 2007). Experiment 1 examined sixty speakers' productions of CVN words and quantified within-speaker normalized coarticulatory vowel nasalization patterns, then related those values to speaking rate variations across utterances. Consistent with what Solé observed in comparing (three) American English speakers' and (three) Continental Spanish speakers' CVVN productions, many of the American English speakers in the current study indeed display "phonological" patterns: since degree of vowel nasalization does not meaningfully vary with speech rate, the implication is that vowel nasalization is a targeted, deliberate aspect of these speakers' productions and suggests phonologization of coarticulatory vowel nasalization. This relationship was observed on average, based on aggregated analysis.

However, we observed a great deal of across-speaker variation in the relationship between speech rate and degree of coarticulatory nasalization. Individuals who produced a positive "trade-off" relationship between temporal organization of segments and degree of coarticulatory vowel nasalization could be classified as "mechanical" speakers: paralleling what was found for Spanish, these speakers' vowel nasalization patterns appear timed to the nasal coda consonant such that the velum lowering gesture exerted less or more of an extent as speech rate increased or decreased, respectively. Individuals who showed nonprosodically determined nasal coarticulation were classified as having "phonologized" coarticulation. We also identified a third speaker classi- fication where many displayed a negative relationship between speech rate and degree of coarticulatory vowel nasality. Such a scenario is consistent with a *local hyperarticulation* strategy, wherein slower speaking rates involve a reorganization of coarticulatory extent to provide enhanced cues to the nasal coda (Avelino et al., 2020; de Jong, 2004; Scarborough, 2013; Scarborough & Zellou, 2013). However, unlike what has previously been observed for English and Korean on average, where words containing longer vowels under stress receive less nasal coarticulation (Cho et al., 2017; Jang et al., 2018; Zellou & Scarborough, 2012), enhancers display increased nasal coarticulation as speech rate gets slower. This is similar to what has been reported in Kakataibo where words with nasal consonants are produced with increased nasal coarticulation when in prosodically strong positions (Avelino et al., 2020). Such a scenario has been observed within speakers based on communicative context (Scarborough & Zellou, 2013). Therefore, it is possible that the variation in strategy for certain individuals has some functionally oriented explanation, motivation, or origin.

One notable difference between the studies done by Solé and that reported here, is that Solé explicitly elicited differences in speaking rates within individ- uals (in one condition, Solé instructed participants to speak very slowly while in another condition they were instructed to speak very fast). In the present study, we did not elicit extreme variations in speaking rate. Yet, speakers did naturally vary their speaking rate across utterances and this overall replicated the aggre- gate pattern for American English, and allowed us to further categorize individ- uals as meaningfully different in their coarticulation repertoires. Thus, it is promising to observe that the Solé approach is generalizable without explicitly eliciting different speaking rates. Examining cross-speaker differences in coar- ticulation repertoires using this approach, while also eliciting a larger range in speaking rate styles within speakers, is a promising direction for future work.

Overall, then, we find further evidence for individual differences in speaker- specific coarticulatory repertoires. This is consistent with proposals in recent work that speakers have unique articulatory-gestural representations for coar- ticulation that vary from the community mean in idiosyncratic ways (Beddor, 2009; Yu & Zellou, 2019; Zellou, 2017). Prior researchers have categorized American English has having "phonologized" vowel nasalization (Solé, 2007);

while the present results do support this as being the community norm for American English speakers (twenty-three of sixty speakers were categorized as such), we also observe a great deal of variation across speakers. Sixteen of sixty speakers show patterns consistent with "mechanical" coarticulation.

The distinct cross-speaker anticipatory coarticulation repertoires, and the classification of these patterns in *phonological* terms, opens the question of how are these variable talkers perceived? More specifically, can we use a perceptual evaluation of the vowels produced by these talkers to further substantiate the claims that some within English produce grammar-specified coarticulatory vowel nasalization and others do not? In Experiment 2, we investigate this question.

3 Experiment 2: Quantifying Individual Differences in Phonologization in Perception

Experiment 1 outlined an approach to typologize American English speakers as either displaying phonologized coarticulatory vowel nasality in CVN words or not, using the acoustic signal. In Experiment 2, we aim to perform a perceptual assessment of these categorizations, using listeners' phonological classifications of the sixty speakers' vowels.

The representational status of coarticulatory vowel nasality was explored using listeners' perceptual responses by Lahiri and Marslen-Wilson (1991), who advocated for an underspecification view of coarticulatory features in lexical storage and retrieval. To test their view, they presented truncated [CṼ] and [CV] syllables, which had been excised from CVN and CVC contexts respectively, to English-speaking listeners. They also examined perception of truncated syllables in Bengali, where vowels can be phonemically, as well as coarticulatorily, nasalized (e.g., [bad] "difference," [bãn] "flood," [bãd] "dam"). Their underspecification hypothesis led them to predict distinct patterns of lexical identifications from truncated syllables with oral and nasalized vowels across the two languages. First, for nasalized vowels in English, while they argue that underspecification does not imply that CVN words are stored with nasalized vowels in the English lexicon, vowel nasalization might be a perceptual cue for upcoming sounds. Thus, they predict that English [CṼ] could be identified as CVN. In Bengali, nasalization is contrastive, so they predict that [CṼ] will be identified overwhelmingly as CṼC, whether it originated from CVN or CṼC words. For oral vowels, Lahiri and Marslen-Wilson predicted that [CV] syllables are allowed to be interpreted as CVN lexical items; since vowels are not specified as [nasal], an oral vowel does not provide listeners with cues supporting either a CVC or CVN interpretation conclusively. Thus, an underspecification hypothesis would predict that [CV] will be ambiguous to English and Bengali listeners.

However, Ohala and Ohala (1995) advocate for a phonetic representation view, where listeners store forms of words encoded with fine phonetic detail from experience. Under the phonetic representation hypothesis, the absence of vowel nasalization in [CV] is predicted to be just as informative as the presence of vowel nasalization; therefore, [CṼ] syllables should be identified as CVN items and [CV] syllables identified as CVC items unambiguously. Also, Ohala and Ohala critiqued the Lahiri and Marslen-Wilson (1991) study and replicated it with several key methodological changes (their study also happened to use Hindi, a language with a similar oral-nasal vowel contrast to Bengali). First, in the original study, participants' responses were open-choice (free response). Ohala and Ohala (1995) argued that this design feature could have limited listeners' use of speech variation to perceive the *contrast* between oral and nasalized vowels. Furthermore, they argued that presenting the syllables truncated into silence could have created auditory perceptions of oral stops in word-final position. Thus, Ohala and Ohala designed a forced-choice task and also gated the stimuli into noise in order to mitigate a bias toward perceiving an oral coda stop.

Table 3 provides a summary of the response proportions reported by Lahiri and Marslen-Wilson (1991) and Ohala and Ohala (1995) for English and Table 4 summarizes the results from both studies for Bengali and Hindi, respectively. Bolded values indicate the response type with the highest response proportion for each stimulus type. For both languages and both studies, [CV] syllables were identified as CVC the most often. In Bengali/Hindi, [CṼ] syllables from both CVN and CṼC words were identified as CṼC in both studies. Where the studies diverged, however, was in English listeners' response patterns to [CṼ] syllables in English. Ohala and Ohala found evidence

Table 3 Summary of percentages of word-type responses for English [CV] and [CṼ] stimuli at vowel offset across the Lahiri and Marslen-Wilson and Ohala and Ohala studies.

		Response Proportion			
		Lahiri and Marlslen-Wilson's (1991) open choice task [taken from table 3]		Ohala and Ohala's (1995) 2-option forced choice task [taken from table 4.7]	
English Stimuli		*CVC*	*CVN*	*CVC*	*CVN*
Stim. Type	[CV](C)	**83%**	16.6%	**79%**	21%
	[CṼ](N)	**59.3%**	40.7%	17.9%	**82.1%**

Phonology

Table 4 Summary of percentages of word-type responses for Bengali/Hindi [CV] and [CṼ] stimuli at vowel offset across the Lahiri and Marslen-Wilson (Bengali) and Ohala and Ohala (Hindi) studies.

		Response Proportion					
		Lahiri and Marlslen-Wilson's (1991) open choice task for Bengali [taken from table 2]			Ohala and Ohala's (1995) 3-option forced choice task for Hindi [taken from table 4.5]		
Bengali/Hindi Stimuli		CVC	CVN	CṼC	CVC	CVN	CṼC
Stim.	[CV](C)	80.3%	13.4%	0.7%	**71.8%**	8.7%	19.5%
Type	[CṼ](N)	23.5%	7.9%	**56.8%**	19.9%	24.4%	**55.8%**
	[CṼ](C)	33.2%	5.2%	**63%**	14.4%	14.4%	**71.3%**

that English listeners identify [CṼ] as signaling CVN words, supporting the phonetic representation hypothesis, while Lahiri and Marslen-Wilson (1991) found a higher CVC response rate for these stimuli, which they argue supports the possibility that vowel nasalization is underspecified in English.

Another theoretical point Lahiri and Marslen-Wilson (1991) raise is the possible influence of gradient differences in patterns of vowel nasality. They say that evidence that listeners use gradient coarticulatory information would be reflected in differences in lexical identification related to differences in degree of vowel nasalization. Though they do not find evidence for this hypothesis, it still remains an open question that was not investigated further in either Lahiri and Marslen-Wilson (1991) or Ohala and Ohala (1995).

Experiment 2 was designed to revisit the question of how coarticulatory vowel nasalization is represented using the theoretical and methodological approaches of these studies. Using the refined paradigm of Ohala and Ohala (1995), we presented truncated [CṼ] and [CV] syllables (gated into noise) from all of the sixty speakers from Experiment 1 to listeners who performed forced-choice lexical categorizations (either CVC or CVN). In particular, we use this methodology, and the competing predictions outlined by the prior studies, to test questions about variation across these sixty speakers.

First, we ask whether there is variation across speakers in listeners' ability to access the intended phonological structure of a truncated CV syllable. For one, neither Lahiri and Marslen-Wilson or Ohala and Ohala raise the possibility that there might be variation across speakers. We hold that this paradigm is essentially a way to perceptually define differences in grammars for coarticulatory vowel nasalization that might exist across speakers. In particular, the cross-language comparison in both studies found strong evidence that in a language with phonologized vowel nasalization, listeners are able to categorize oral and nasalized vowels as signaling distinct lexical categories. On the other hand, there is weaker evidence (variation across studies) in whether vowel nasalization signals a CVN lexical item in a nonnasal contrastive language. In effect, we test whether these patterns can be used to identify variation across speakers of English in the phonological realization of the CVC versus CVN contrast.

Secondly, we aim to relate variation across perceptual evaluation of speakers to the production-based classifications made in Experiment 1. Specifically, if listeners' categorization of coarticulation reflects the phonological specification of vowel nasalization, then we predict that CVN categorizations will be highest for nasalized vowels produced by the speakers classified as having "phonologized" coarticulatory patterns. Along the same lines, nasalized vowels produced by "mechanical" coarticulators should have the lowest CVN categorizations since those speakers' nasalization patterns ostensibly originate from low-level articulatory processes, rather than grammatically relevant ones. Speakers who produce "enhancement" coarticulation should also have high CVN categorizations, but only when coarticulatory patterns are hyperarticulated (e.g., tokens with the greatest amount of nasalization).

3.1 Methods

3.1.1 Participants

Ninety-four University of California–Davis undergraduates participated in this study (eighty-four female, ten male; age range = 18–28 years old, average age = 19.9 years old), recruited through the UC Davis psychology subject pool, none of whom had participated in Experiment 1. All were native speakers of American English and received course credit for their participation. None reported any visual or hearing impairment.

3.1.2 Materials and Procedure

Stimuli for Experiment 2 consisted of CV syllables truncated from the CVC and CVN word productions by the sixty speakers from Experiment 1. In order to keep the experiment a reasonable length, only the first production of each word from the frame sentence was used in Experiment 2. The syllables were then gated into wide-band noise, at a level 5 dB less than the peak intensity of the vowel in order to avoid a stop-bias that might occur with the syllables abruptly ending in silence (i.e., similar to the method used by Ohala & Ohala, 1995).

Participants completed a word completion task. This task was designed to have a procedure similar to the paradigm used by Ohala and Ohala (1995). On a given trial, listeners heard one of the speakers produce either a [CV] syllable (truncated from CVC) or a [CṼ] syllable (truncated from CVN) gated into noise. Then, listeners selected which one of two minimal pair choices (either a CVC or CVN, corresponding to the minimal pair option for that syllable) the syllable was extracted from.

3.2 Results

Listener responses were coded for accurately selecting the correct minimal pair item originally produced in a trial (1) or not (0). Aggregated lexical identification of items across speakers is above chance performance for both [CV] (93 percent) and [CṼ] (72 percent) syllables. These overall rates are similar to those reported by Ohala and Ohala (1995) and support the hypothesis that listeners encode phonetic detail to both orality and nasality such that information on the vowel alone reliably cues the lexical distinction between CVC and CVN words. The extremely high accuracy for [CV] (oral vowel) syllables suggests that oral vowels are unambiguous; this is consistent with Ohala and Ohala's claim that oral vowels are a result of a "feature spreading" of an oral feature – or, at least, that oral vowels are specified for orality. This interpretation is contra Lahiri and Marslen-Wilson's hypothesis that oral vowels are ambiguous in English and that a lack of vowel nasality leaves open either a CVC or CVN identification. The average identification rate for [CṼ] syllables is also higher than chance, again in line with the hypothesis that nasalized vowels are specified for nasality such that listeners are able to identify the correct lexical category based on the vowel alone. However, the higher performance for [CV] versus [CṼ] does suggest that nasalized vowels are more ambiguous than oral vowels. This supports proposals that the acoustic properties of nasalization make vowels more perceptually ambiguous (Beddor, 1993; Wright, 1986).

Indeed, these aggregate patterns are consistent with those reported in Ohala and Ohala (1995). However, as seen in Figure 7, which provides the by-speaker mean proportion correct word identification for oral and nasalized vowel syllables, there is a considerable amount of variation across speakers in the likelihood of listeners to identify the intended phonological structure. While there is variation across speakers for both oral and nasalized vowels, as seen in Figure 7, there is a larger range of variation for nasalized vowels (speaker mean accuracy range = 25–98 percent CVN identification) than for oral vowels (speaker mean accuracy range = 71–98 percent CVC identification). This asymmetry in range of variation across oral and nasalized vowels suggests

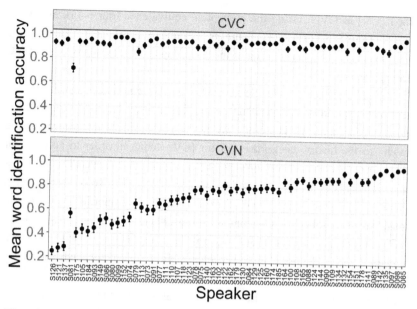

Figure 7 By-speaker means and standard errors for proportion of CV syllables correctly identified. The top panel displays responses for syllables extracted from CVC contexts; the bottom panel displays responses for syllables from CVN contexts.

that there is more variation across speakers in the realization of nasality than orality, in expressing the phonological contrast between CVC and CVN words.

Furthermore, we can investigate what the differences across speakers' mean identification of [CṼ] stimuli suggest for differing hypotheses about coarticulation being lexically specified. For instance, S126's [CṼ]s were only identified as CVN 25 percent of the time; put differently, [CṼ] for this talker was rated 75 percent of the time as CVC. This talker's identification patterns (and those with similar rates for [CṼ]), then, are actually consistent with an interpretation that their oral and nasalized vowels are "phonologically equivalent" in that, based on the vowel alone, listeners hear vowels as oral only. On the other hand, some talkers produce nasal coarticulated vowels that are phonologically ambiguous; that is, mean identification rates for [CṼ] syllables are around chance level (50 percent, such as S152). These speakers produce oral and nasalized vowels in a way that is consistent with Lahiri and Marslen-Wilson's (1991) prediction that coarticulated vowels are underspecified for nasality, such that their acoustic realization provides cues to both CVC and CVN lexical items equally. Meanwhile, some talkers receive over 90 percent accuracy in listeners' identification of their [CṼ] as CVN. Using the perceptual equivalence framework again, we can interpret these speakers' patterns as indicating robust use of phonetic features in the lexical encoding of the phonological distinction between CVC and CVN words.

We predicted that the variable realization of nasal coarticulation across items and across speakers might explain differences in phonological categorizations observed in Figure 6. Therefore, we ran a mixed effects logistic regression model to the binary categorizations for [CṼ] items. In order to account for token-specific coarticulatory properties, the degree of vowel nasalization measured in each vowel was included as a fixed effect. This Vowel Nasalization value was selected to be the normalized nasalization proportion score, calculated for each token in Experiment 1 (described in Section 2.1.4), at the midpoint of the vowel. Note that this was the same timepoint used in the final statistical model reported in Experiment 1. In addition, for each token, the speaker's classification from Experiment 1 (treatment coded: Mechanical [reference level], Phonologized, Enhancement) was added to the model. The model also included by-listener random intercepts and by-listener slopes for both main effects. Model syntax: *glmer(Categorization Accuracy ~ Vowel Nasalization + Speaker Classification + (1 + Vowel Nasalization + Speaker Classification | Listener))*.

The model revealed a main effect of Vowel Nasalization wherein listeners were more likely to categorize tokens that contained greater degree of coarticulatory vowel nasality as CVN lexical items [$Coef = 2.05$, $SE = 0.13$, $z = 15.56$, $p < 0.001$].

Above and beyond the contribution of the coarticulatory patterns within a given token, the model also revealed that speaker classification also predicted categorization of nasalized syllables. Figure 8 provides the mean CVN categorization proportions for [CṼ] syllables by speaker classification type. As seen, listeners were more likely to categorize nasalized vowels as phonologically CVN for the Phonologized speakers, compared to the Mechanical speakers [$Coef = 0.44$, $SE = 0.07$, $z = 6.63$, $p < 0.001$]. Meanwhile, relative to the Mechanical speakers, listeners were less likely to categorize Enhancement speakers' nasalized vowels as CVN [$Coef = -0.55$, $SE = 0.07$, $z = -8.45$, $p < 0.001$].

3.3 Experiment 2 Interim Discussion

The results from Experiment 2 provide evidence for individual variation in the phonological specification of coarticulatory vowel nasalization. First, oral vowels are overwhelmingly accurately categorized as CVC lexical items, and

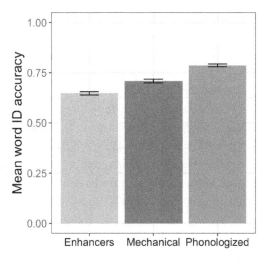

Figure 8 Means and standard errors for proportion of syllables with nasalized correctly identified aggregated over speaker categories.

there was little cross-talker variation in oral vowel categorization patterns. This can be taken as evidence that American English listeners store and use the absence of nasalization to identify words with oral codas. Secondly, nasalized vowels are also not technically ambiguous, in the aggregate. This is consistent with theoretical proposals that listeners also store and use coarticulatory information present on vowels alone to identify phonological structure of words (Ohala & Ohala, 1995). However, we observe a large amount of variation in rates of CVN identification across speakers' [CṼ] productions. Notably, the between-speaker variation in categorization of nasalized vowels as CVN is considerable (Figure 7) – it is much larger than the variation within talkers. Thus, the realization of coarticulatory nasalization in American English is highly speaker specific.

We explored whether acoustic properties of the speakers' productions of nasal-coarticulated vowels could explain cross-speaker differences in phonological identification. Talker-specific variation in extent of anticipatory nasal coarticulation has been observed (Zellou, 2017). With respect to token-specific properties, we found that degree of vowel nasalization present on each nasalized vowel predicted CVN identification: vowels that were more nasalized were more likely to be categorized as a CVN lexical item. This aligns with prior work that listeners are sensitive to gradient variations in coarticulatory nasalization and use it to make lexical predictions about words (Beddor et al., 2013; and also Zellou & Dahan, 2019). This is consistent with the proposal that listeners are sensitive to gradient phonetic cues to phonological information (Kleinschmidt & Jaeger, 2015; McMurray & Jongman, 2011; McMurray et al., 2002). Here, we find that probabilistic cues to CVN word identity present on the vowels varies systematically across speakers.

Furthermore, we found that the classifications of speakers from Experiment 1, based on their idiosyncratic relationship between prosodic structure and coarticulatory extent, having either "mechanical," "enhancing," or "phonologized" coarticulatory vowel nasalization also predicted listeners' likelihood of correctly identifying the intended phonological structure of words based on only hearing the nasalized vowels. Above and beyond the effect of item-specific nasalization patterns, we found that speaker-specific classifications, based on the overall relationship between speech rate and coarticulatory degree, also predicted listeners' ability to categorize nasalized vowels as phonologically CVN. Listeners were *better* able to perform CVN categorizations for speakers who displayed more "phonologized" prosodic-coarticulatory patterns, on average, than speakers who displayed more "mechanical" prosodic-coarticulatory patterns. Since "phonologized" speakers display more targeted and deliberate coarticulatory features, not determined by temporal-prosodic changes, this appears to facilitate listener identification of CVN words based on their vowels alone. Meanwhile, speakers appear to be less able to use the coarticulatory information as meaningful for the "mechanical" speakers since they display greater temporally conditioned coarticulation. This extends the work of those who have looked at the temporal-coarticulation relationship as a way of comparing different languages (e.g., Solé, 2007) to speakers and, further, to listeners' perceptual-phonological assessment of those typologies. The classification of the 1:1 relationship between nasal coarticulation and vowel duration changes as being phonologized can also be supported in the domain of speech perception.

With respect to models of sound change, diachronically, /CṼ/ is argued to be preceded by a /CṼN/ stage (Beddor, 2009; Ohala, 1993). Here, we find evidence that some American English speakers indeed produce words that can be acoustically and perceptually represented as /CṼN/. Moreover, the comparison of the phonologized and mechanical speakers' perceptual assessment also provides support for hybrid speaker-listener based models of pathways of historical variation (Beddor, 2009). Specifically, we find that both the speakers' patterns and the listeners' behavior in being sensitive to those patterns are components of a phonetically nasalized vowel being perceived as inherently encoding the phonological feature [+nasal]. It also supports Beddor's (2009) proposal that listeners are sensitive to the *dynamics* of coarticulation and the *precise nature* of coarticulatory variation; in the current study, this relates to listeners' sensitivity to speaker-specific relationships between prosodic structure and coarticulation.

One surprising aspect of the results of Experiment 2 was that listeners were least likely to identify nasalized vowels produced by "enhancement" speakers as CVNs, relative to the other types of speakers. For those speakers, the relationship between coarticulatory nasality and prosodic structure was systematic, like the "mechanical" speakers, yet it was in the reverse direction. Enhancement speakers produced greater nasalization in utterances where their speech rate was slower. This was dubbed an enhancement strategy because prior work has found that a positive relationship between vowel duration and degree of coarticulatory nasalization mitigates perceptual difficulty of highly confusable words (Scarborough & Zellou, 2013). However, since speakers who received this classification did not result in greater identification of the excised nasal coda, perhaps this label is inaccurate. Another possibility is that in enhancing, other acoustic-phonetic features could be covarying, which might make the vowels more difficult to identify as CVN. This is a possibility that is ripe to be explored in future work.

While Experiment 2 only looked at one acoustic characteristic associated with nasal coarticulation, there are other phonetic features that covary with degree of coarticulatory vowel nasalization. Recent studies have identified distinct tongue positions associated with nasalized vowels in American English, suggesting that nasalized vowels are phonologized with distinct oral articulations (Carignan, 2011, 2014; Zellou & Scarborough, 2019). Future work can explore cross-speaker variations in oral articulations for nasalized and nonnasalized vowels, and its perceptual consequences.

Thus, across Experiments 1 and 2, we find both acoustic and perceptual definitions for the ways in which individual speakers vary in their phonological grammars for coarticulatory vowel nasalization. In the next section, the results from both experiments are further discussed with respect to this claim and broader theoretical issues regarding the representational status of coarticulatory vowel nasalization.

4 General Discussion and Future Directions

How are phonetic details represented in the minds of speakers? This question can inform phonological theory since it concerns the type of knowledge that language users have about how to produce and understand the legal words of their language. Coarticulatory details, in particular, have taken center stage in this discussion, for several reasons. For one, coarticulation is a type of context-dependent variation. In models of phonology that strongly assume underspecification of phonetic details, coarticulation has been explained as a consequence of the mechanical nature of speech production; similarly, compensatory perceptual processes have been taken as evidence that listeners "subtract" coarticulation when comprehending the speech signal, resulting in mental forms for words that are devoid of acoustic-phonetic information. Yet, in phonetic-specification approaches, coarticulatory patterns are observed to vary in systematic ways across languages and communicative contexts, indicating that speakers have rich knowledge about how coarticulatory variation is used in their language. Experimental examination of how listeners behave in response to carefully controlled utterances also supports the view that coarticulatory variation is used in the online comprehension of lexical items. Another reason why coarticulation has been so prominent in discussions of phonological theory is its role in explaining common historical sound changes. One classic approach takes a view that "today's alternation was yesterday's sound change," whereby researchers have pointed out that many synchronic within-language phonological patterns (e.g., oral vs. nasalized vowels; vowel harmony systems, consonant epenthesis) have historical origins in coarticulatory variation (Blevins, 2004; Ohala, 1993). More specifically, an individual's reanalysis of coarticulatory details from having a biomechanical source to being intended and deliberate has been proposed to be a mechanism by which phonetic variation can become phonologized as grammatically relevant (Ohala, 1993).

The experiments in the current work were designed to speak to both of these theoretical questions about coarticulation (i.e., how it is represented in synchronic grammars and its role in historical sound changes). Coarticulation is a complex phenomenon, which requires careful consideration of several factors. In particular, prior research has identified ways in which speakers and listeners across different languages vary in their coarticulatory behavior. For production, one proposal has been that coarticulatory patterns can be classified in terms of the relationship between prosodic organization and patterning of coarticulation in order to determine whether coarticulatory vowel nasalization is grammatically specified (e.g., such as that observed on the aggregate for English) or mechanical (e.g., observed for Spanish) (Solé, 2007). In Experiment 1 in the present Element, the acoustic characteristics of vowels in preoral and prenasal contexts produced by sixty American English speakers was examined. Using Solé's approach to categorizing languages as having either "mechanical" or "phonologized" coarticulatory nasalization, we related variation in speech rate and degree of vowel nasalization within the sixty talkers' productions of CVN words. We observe extensive cross-talker variation in the realization of coarticulatory vowel nasality. We identified that within these sixty speakers, some could be classified as having more "phonologized" coarticulatory patterns, while some had more "mechanical" coarticulatory patterns. Some speakers had a third type, which we labeled "enhancement" since they produced greater coarticulation in more careful speaking rates; this can be related to coarticulatory patterns reported in some languages (e.g., in Kakataibo, Avelino et al. (2020)). Thus, we found synchronic, within-language variation across speakers that reflect that cross-language, diachronic patterns that has been described. This finding is consistent with the idea that there is individual variation in phonological grammars (e.g., Beddor, 2009; Yu & Zellou, 2019) and provides a quantifiable way to categorize heterogeneity within a speech community in this respect. From this view, individual variation is not "noise" but rather it is an essential part of synchronic variation. These findings also are consistent with notions about the dynamics of historical change, supporting the view that individual variation in a speech community represents the pool of synchronic variation as the source of historical change (Beddor, 2009; Blevins, 2004; Lindblom et al., 1995; Ohala, 1993).

In Experiment 2, we took the oral and nasalized vowels from the sixty speakers from Experiment 1 and had an independent group of listeners categorize them as either CVC or CVN words. This perceptual assessment of these oral and nasalized vowels is another approach to classify individual variation in the phonologization of coarticulation across speakers: High performance in identifying a speaker's [CṼ] syllables as CVN lexical items can be interpreted as a reflecting that speaker is advanced in the phonologization of nasal coarticulation; Low performance indicates a speaker who produces weak coarticulation such that it does not provide robust cues to lexical identity. Again, prior work has established this as a way to explore the representational status of vowel nasalization across languages: English-speaking listeners have been shown to display more variable patterns in identifying coarticulated vowels as signaling lexical nasality, while Bengali and Hindi listeners (languages with contrastive vowel nasalization) have been shown to display more reliable across studies in hearing vowel nasalization as signaling a [+ nasal] contrastive feature (Lahiri & Marslen-Wilson, 1991; Ohala & Ohala, 1995). Overall, we observe strong evidence for phonetic specification for orality across all speakers indicating that American English vowels in oral consonant contexts are grammatically represented as oral, consistent with what has been argued in prior work (Ohala & Ohala, 1995). Furthermore, we also find a huge range of cross-speaker variation in how reliably [CṼ] vowels were categorized as CVN in American English. Some talkers' [CṼ] syllables are ambiguous – listeners are unable to reliably identify these talkers' vowels as signaling the nasal contrast. Other talkers produce highly distinctive nasalized vowels and the oral-nasal coda contrast is carried within the preceding vowel alone. This variation cannot be accounted for by saying that American English has a strictly underrepresented or phonetically specified coarticulatory vowel nasalization status; rather, the grammatical status of coarticulatory vowel nasalization varies by speaker.

The variation seen within American English, across speakers, has parallels in cross-language typological coarticulatory patterns: some speakers produce nasalized vowels that are categorized more often as CVC, indicating they are realized as phonetically equivalent to oral vowels, while some speakers produce vowels that are unequivocally identified as CVN, suggesting phonologically nasal vowels. This supports proposals that a speech community contains a large amount of variation in the extent to which coarticulation is used as a cue to lexical contrast and that variation is the pool from which novel sound variants are selected.

Moreover, the classification from Experiment 1 of speakers as having phonologized, mechanical, or enhancement coarticulation also predicted likelihood of CVN categorization in Experiment 2, above and beyond the token-specific coarticulatory patterns. Speakers who had been categorized as having phonologized coarticulatory patterns produced nasalized vowels that were more likely to be categorized as CVN than mechanical speakers. This is consistent with the notion that phonologized coarticulation is deliberate and reflects active maintenance of coarticulatory cues on the vowel (Solé, 2007). Nasalized vowels from speakers classified as having phonologized coarticulation were most likely to be heard as linguistically nasal by listeners. This finding is consistent with Beddor's (2009) hybrid speaker- and listener-oriented model of coarticulatory-mediated sound change. Speakers who actively maintain and target vowel nasality produce vowels that are easy for listeners to phonologically classify as nasal. Thus, these observations dovetail with the hypothesis that both the speakers and the listeners play a role in the phonologization of coarticulation. This is additional evidence that reflexes of cross-linguistic coarticulatory patterns, both in production and perception, occur within American English, across speakers.

However, contrary to our predictions, we find that listeners displayed the lowest likelihood of CVN categorization for speakers who produced "enhancing" patterns of nasal coarticulation. Speakers classified as "enhancers" produced increasing coarticulatory extent with slower speech rates. An increase in coarticulation as a function of hyperarticulation can be seen as an adaptive variation (Beddor, 2009; Lindblom et al., 1995; Scarborough, 2013). While we did find that vowels containing a greater extent of coarticulatory nasalization are identified as CVN more often, consistent with prior work (Beddor et al., 2013; Scarborough & Zellou, 2013), perhaps there is something particular about the phonetic patterns of "enhancers" that make their nasalized vowel productions less easy for listeners to categorize as CVN. Relating our goal of examining speaker-specific coarticulatory patterns that have analogs in cross-linguistic variation, a parallel might be drawn between such an "enhancement" strategy and the proposal that cross-linguistic variation in coarticulatory patterns varies as a function of whether that feature plays a role in lexical contrast within that language (e.g., Manuel, 1990). Since consistent evidence for such a strong link has been equivocal, it makes sense that speakers who adopt a more functionally oriented strategy might produce vowels that are easily identifiable as phonologically nasal. Future work can provide a more in-depth investigation and understanding of what type of speaker might adopt this "enhancement" strategy.

The phonetic implementation of nasalization is a gradient phenomenon in Experiment 1. This finding is consistent with models that argue that phonetic properties can be represented both in terms of universal articulatory properties and grammatical/stored properties of sounds (Cho & Ladefoged, 1999). Moreover, we can extend this to cross-speaker variation: every speaker produces coarticulatory vowel nasalization, but speakers vary systematically from each other reflecting differences in how individual speakers learn and control the degree and timing of coarticulatory vowel nasalization. This is consistent with prior work demonstrating that individual speakers vary in the weighting of coarticulatory nasalization as a produced cue to an upcoming nasal consonant (Beddor, 2009).

We also find that the perceptual patterns in Experiment 2 are gradient. For perception, we find that the perception of coarticulatory vowel nasalization in English is linear, not step-like; listeners' use of acoustic cues for vowel nasalization is gradient (Beddor et al., 2013; Zellou & Dahan, 2019), like acoustic cues to other contrasts (e.g., VOT in McMurray et al., 2002). Thus, this study emphasizes the importance of understanding the relationship between controlled, deliberate phonetic implementation of noncontrastive variation and how that can be used to signal linguistic meaning. It supports theories of representation that pose more gradient and fine-grained phonetic details to be stored in the memory traces of words (Pierrehumbert, 2016). Probabilistic models of phoneme processing can also account for this observation (Kleinschmidt & Jaeger, 2015; McMurray & Jongman, 2011). Bayesian approaches to speech perception propose that probabilistic perceptual processing is beneficial to listeners because it allows them to quickly adapt if they come across counterevidence to phoneme categorizations (Clayards et al., 2008; McMurray et al., 2002; Zellou & Dahan, 2019). That speakers show gradient variation and listeners, in turn, display similarly gradient sensitivity to the coarticulatory cues perhaps allows for listeners to be flexible and adapt to variation in within-category differences in CVN realization.

The findings that within a speech community there is intraspeaker variation in how coarticulation is grammatically represented have implications for models of sound change. For one, these observations support a scenario where multiple types of phonological grammars across speakers within a speech community are encountered by a listener. The variation in speaker-specific grammars is relevant for understanding the nature of historical change. Ohala (1993), for instance, proposes that reanalysis of /VN/ as /ṼN/ is abrupt. Indeed, the commonly proposed pathway of phonologization of coarticulation is VN > ṼN > Ṽ (Ruhlen, 1978). However, our cross-speaker variation indicates that within this dialect of American English, there are, synchronically, individuals at both the first and second stage of this pathway. Thus, this appears to be a gradient transition, rather than an abrupt one. Furthermore, it is a common assumption that the /ṼN/ stage (i.e., speaker in the current study who we identified as having the "phonologized" coarticulatory pattern), is the more innovative pattern; hence, that /VN/ is the more conservative pattern (i.e., those speakers we identified as having "mechanical" coarticulation). However, there is some counterevidence in the literature for this unidirectional pathway of grammaticalization. For instance, Zellou and Tamminga (2014) measured the degree of nasal coarticulation for vowels in monosyllabic CVN words from 105 speakers with birthyears ranging from 1949 to 1991 from a naturalistic speech corpus of native Philadelphians. They observed that young adult speakers born between the years of 1950 and 1965 show a trend of producing increasing amounts of coarticulatory vowel nasality, while those born after 1965 trend toward decreasing degree of nasal coarticulation. In light of the observation in the present study that *both* types of speakers can coexist with a synchronic speech community, it cannot be assumed a priori that one type is innovative and the other type is conservative until across-time trends can be identified.

Another aspect of the findings in the current studies also speak to the goal of relating synchronic within-language variation to cross-language patterns. Recall that prior work has reported instances in some languages of more than one level of vowel nasality contrast (Lakota in Scarborough et al., 2015; Palantla Chicatec in Merrifield & Edmonson, 1999 and Blevins, 2004). While the current experiments were not designed to examine sources of multiple grammatical levels of nasalization within-speaker, the cross-speaker patterns support the possibility that distinct patterns of coarticulation could grammaticalize in a speech community independently. In particular, the "enhancement" coarticulation speakers displayed the greatest amount of coarticulatory nasalization in slower speech rates. This could be reanalyzed by individuals who already have a "phonologized" pattern as a distinct and novel type of coarticulatory pattern (or vice-versa), via hypocorrection. Such a possibility is speculation at this point, but future work exploring the interaction between speakers with distinct grammatical patterns is a promising avenue.

The present study also has implications for teaching phonology. For one, several theoretical questions were explored in the Introduction about the relationship between the acoustic signal and the mental representations for speech sounds: what constrains coarticulation?; what types of coarticulation are there and how can we distinguish between them?; why is there variation in coarticulation within a language? We also asked how variation across speakers in a language can be used to understand the types of coarticulation found cross-linguistically and also how coarticulation evolves over time within a language. Appreciating how examining coarticulation can address longstanding questions about the storage and evolution of phonetic patterns in the phonological grammar can enrich phonology pedagogy. Secondly, the present work provides an example of a laboratory approach to understanding and exploring phonological patterns. Relatedly, it provides an example of an empirical demonstration of an approach to investigate how the seeds of cross-linguistic phonological variation in within-language differences across individuals (Beddor, 2009; Ohala, 1993). In this way, teaching phonological theory can be enriched by integrating synchronic and diachronic, comparative sources of evidence. Teaching theoretical phonology can also be enriched by looking at phonological variation in a multidimensional way (Cohn & Renwick, 2021; Zellou & Brotherton, 2021; Zellou & Scarborough, 2019). This was illustrated both with respect to looking at multiple acoustic features in tandem and also integrating data from the production and perception of speech.

While this Element presented multiple studies exploring aspects of individual variation in coarticulatory vowel nasalization, there were many limitations of the current work which provide avenues for future research. For example, while a relationship between individual variation in English and language-specific patterns was made, exploring individual variation in other languages can enhance our understanding of how the "pool of variation" might differ across languages. For example, is English highly flexible, allowing such a large range of variation, because vowel nasalization is not contrastive? Furthermore, the current experiments focused only on California speakers (and listeners) and future work can identify whether the same pattern and variation are found in other varieties of English. Relatedly, another promising future direction is to explore the role of social meaning in explaining cross-speaker variation. Since coarticulatory vowel nasalization can vary to such a large degree across speakers, the extent to which individuals associate variations in nasalization with social-indexical meaning is highly underexplored (cf. Brotherton et al., 2019; Tamminga & Zellou, 2015; Zellou & Tamminga, 2014). In particular, how synthesizing listener-oriented models of coarticulatory-based sound change (e.g., Ohala, 1993) and socio-linguistically based models of sound change is a promising direction for addressing unresolved issues in the actuation and spread of novel phonetic variations (cf. Baker et al., 2011). Additionally, some scholars have even examined whether differences in cognitive processing style, or personality-related factors, across individuals can provide insight into what type of listeners are more likely to initiate coarticulatory-based sound changes (e.g., Yu, 2010; see Yu & Zellou, 2019 for review). One open question for future investigation is whether the three speaker categories identified in the current study correlate with differences in cognitive-personality factors such as those examined in prior work.

Another limitation of the current work is its focus only on nasal coarticulation and only American English. We believe that many of the questions and approaches to coarticulation taken in this study can be applied to other types of coarticulatory phenomena and, of course, across other languages. For instance, work examining other types of coarticulatory properties, such as vowel-to-vowel coarticulation, place-of-articulation coarticulation or sibilant coarticulation, can further expand on how listeners vary in the extent to which they phonologize articulatory overlap in their production grammars. The current work also only focuses on alveolar nasal coarticulation and also did not compare cross-vowel differences. In some cases, sound changes have been documented that involve only velar nasal contexts or only for some vowels (Calamai & Celata, 2018; Hajek & Maeda, 2000; Sampson, 1999). Moreover, as mentioned in Experiment 1, a growing body of literature has identified how other articulatory and phonetic features covary with vowel nasalization, such as oral articulations and voice quality (Carignan, 2017; Garellek et al., 2016; Matisoff, 1975; Ohala, 1974). The present work took a relatively one-dimensional approach to the study of nasal coarticulation, looking only at a single acoustic correlate of vowel nasality, which is admittedly highly simplified (cf., work looking at dozens of acoustic correlates of vowel nasalization in Styler, 2017). Another aspect of anticipatory nasal coarticulation is the trade-off between coarticulatory extent and nasal coda duration (Beddor, 2007, 2009 in American English, and also other languages, e.g., Busà, 2007 for Italian; Demolin, 2007 for Rwandan). A promising future direction is examining how individual variation in additional acoustic and articulatory correlates of coarticulatory vowel nasalization, and their covariation, relates to the production and perception patterns examined in the present study. Future work can take an even more comprehensive approach to nasal coarticulation, in order to contribute to the historical and synchronic understanding of coarticulatory variation.

Finally, the existence of speaker-specific grammars suggests that listeners might track or adapt to idiosyncratic talkers. Talker-specific perceptual learning is a mechanism that is potentially critical in order for a speech community to contain heterogeneity across speakers. There is also a proposal that familiarity with a novel talker's nasality patterns in context is one avenue for sound change. Perceptual learning has been proposed as a potential mechanism for the spread of sound change (Kraljic & Samuel, 2006; Tamminga et al., 2020). Talker-specific exposure allows listeners to learn and adapt to the particular acoustic structure of that talker's speech patterns and potentially encode it in long term representations, potentially leading to change. Supporting evidence that listeners track talker-specific coarticulatory patterns comes from a coarticulatory imitation study performed by Zellou et al. (2017). In that study, all participants shadowed CVN stimuli produced by a model talker with two levels of nasality: a natural and an increased amount of coarticulatory nasality. Shadowers' experience with these distinct coarticulatory levels was manipulated. One group first completed a shadowing block with only the natural coarticulation stimuli and later completed a shadowing block with the increased coarticulation stimuli. A second group completed the study with the reverse order of blocks. In the first block, the shadowing groups behaved differently: those exposed to stimuli with an increased coarticulatory nasality produced greater nasality than those exposed to stimuli with a natural amount of coarticulatory nasality. However, in block 2, both groups produced identical patterns of nasal coarticulation, regardless of the coarticulatory patterns of the most recent exposure. The interpretation for this was that listeners track, and store in memory, the general coarticulatory patterns of the talker. Observed imitation patterns reflect accrual of past experience with that speaker's vowels. Since by the second block, both groups of participants had similar overall experience with the model talker, they were similarly affected by the total patterns of exposure.

Additional evidence that listeners adapt to talker-specific coarticulation patterns in American English comes from Zellou and Ferenc Segedin (2019), where one group of listeners was exposed a talker who produced a shifted vowel-coarticulatory phoneme realization: CVC items contained nasalized vowels (spliced from CVN words) and CVN items contained hyper-nasalized vowels (spliced from NVN words). Another group of listeners was exposed to unshifted words by the talker. After exposure, both groups were presented syllables, produced by the exposure talker and a novel talker, containing a nasalized vowel [CṼ] and were asked to select either a CVC or CVN word that competed the fragment. Results indicate that listeners generated speaker-specific representations for the phonetic-to-word category mapping for vowel nasal-coarticulatory patterns. Listeners who were exposed to the speaker with the category-shift were more likely to categorize that speaker's nasalized vowels as signaling CVC words, but not for the novel talker. This was taken as evidence that listeners adapted to a talker-specific shifted vowel-nasality system signaling a nasal coda lexical contrast.

The findings from the Zellou et al. (2016) and Zellou et al. (2017) phonetic imitation studies and that from the Zellou and Ferenc Segedin (2019) perceptual learning study support the possibility that listeners not only attend to coarticulatory detail automatically but also that they are highly sensitive to and track talker-specific coarticulation patterns. The stance that talker-specific nasal coarticulation patterns are learned is congruent with the well-founded claim that coarticulatory details are perceptually informative and useful to listeners in making decisions about the lexical content of the speech signal in an early and efficient manner (Beddor, 2009; Beddor et al., 2013). Indeed, tracking and learning talker-specific coarticulatory patterns might be considered useful for spoken word comprehension because it allows listeners to predict how a given talker is going to produce a sequence of phonemes in a given context. Future work investigating further the mechanisms for adaptation to talker-specific coarticulatory patterns can be useful in exploring the proposal that perceptual adaptation is a pathway to sound change. Another unexplored aspect of this question is the relationship between cross-talker generalization of adaptation and the spread of sound change (Tamminga et al., 2020). Since cross-talker adaptation involves the recognition of community-level phonetic norms, this might be more revealing in understanding when listeners adapt to idiosyncratic talker patterns or when they create a more abstract representation for a novel phonetic realization for coarticulation.

References

Ali, L., Gallagher, T., Goldstein, J., & Daniloff, R. (1971). Perception of coarticulated nasality. *The Journal of the Acoustical Society of America*, **49**(2B), 538–540.

Avelino, H., Zariquiey, R., & Pérez-Silva, J. I. (2020). Nasal coarticulation and prosody in Kakataibo. *Phonetica*, **77**(1), 29–54.

Baese-Berk, M., & Goldrick, M. (2009). Mechanisms of interaction in speech production. *Language and Cognitive Processes*, **24**(4), 527–554.

Baker, A., Archangeli, D., & Mielke, J. (2011). Variability in American English s-retraction suggests a solution to the actuation problem. *Language Variation and Change*, **23**(3), 347–374.

Bates, D., Maechler, M., Bolker, B., Walker, S., Bojesen Christensen, R. H., & Singmann, H. (2016). Lme4: Linear mixed-effects models using Eigen and S4. R package version 1.0–6. 2014.

Beddor, P. S. (1993). The perception of nasal vowels. In M. K. Huffman and R. A. Krakow, eds., *Nasals, Nasalization, and the Velum*. New York: Academic Press, pp. 171–196.

Beddor, P. S. (2007). Nasals and nasalization: The relation between segmental and coarticulatory timing. In *Proceedings of the 16th International Congress of Phonetic Sciences (ICPhS 2007)*, pp. 249–254.

Beddor, P. S. (2009). A coarticulatory path to sound change. *Language*, **85**(4), 785–821.

Beddor, P. S. (2015). The relation between language users' perception and production repertoires. In *Proceedings of the 18th International Congress of Phonetic Sciences (ICPhS 2015)*, pp. 1–9.

Beddor, P. S., & Krakow, R. A. (1999). Perception of coarticulatory nasalization by speakers of English and Thai: Evidence for partial compensation. *The Journal of the Acoustical Society of America*, **106**(5), 2868–2887.

Beddor, P. S., Harnsberger, J. D., & Lindemann, S. (2002). Language-specific patterns of vowel-to-vowel coarticulation: Acoustic structures and their perceptual correlates. *Journal of Phonetics*, **30**(4), 591–627.

Beddor, P. S., McGowan, K. B., Boland, J. E., Coetzee, A. W., & Brasher, A. (2013). The time course of perception of coarticulation. *The Journal of the Acoustical Society of America*, **133**(4), 2350–2366.

Blevins, J. (2004). *Evolutionary Phonology: The Emergence of Sound Patterns*. Cambridge: Cambridge University Press.

Blevins, J. (2015). Evolutionary phonology: A holistic approach to sound change typology. In P. Honeybone and J. Salmons, eds., *The Oxford Handbook of Historical Phonology*. Oxford: Oxford University Press, pp. 485–500.

Boberg, C., & Strassel, S. M. (2000). Short-a in Cincinnati: A change in progress. *Journal of English Linguistics*, **28**(2), 108–126.

Bradlow, A. R., & Bent, T. (2002). The clear speech effect for non-native listeners. *The Journal of the Acoustical Society of America*, **112**(1), 272–284.

Bradlow, A. R., Kraus, N., & Hayes, E. (2003). Speaking clearly for children with learning disabilities: Sentence perception in noise. *Journal of Speech, Language, and Hearing Research*, **46**(1), 80–97.

Brotherton, C., Cohn, M., Zellou, G., & Barreda, S. (2019). Sub-regional variation in positioning and degree of nasalization of /æ/ allophones in California. In *Proceedings of the 19th International Congress of Phonetic Sciences (ICPhS 2019)*, pp. 2373–2377.

Busà, M. G. (2007). Coarticulatory nasalization and phonological developments: Data from Italian and English nasal-fricative sequences. In M.-J. Solé, P. S. Beddor, and J. J. Ohala, eds., *Experimental Approaches to Phonology*. Oxford: Oxford University Press, pp. 155–174.

Calamai, S., & Celata, C. (2018). Velar nasals in sound change. On the phonetic origin of Florentine anaphonesis. In D. Recasens and F. Sánchez-Miret, eds., *Production and Perception Mechanisms in Sound Change*. Berlin: Lincom Europa, pp. 39–54.

Carignan, C. (2014). An acoustic and articulatory examination of the "oral" in "nasal": The oral articulations of French nasal vowels are not arbitrary. *Journal of Phonetics*, **46**, 23–33.

Carignan, C. (2017). Covariation of nasalization, tongue height, and breathiness in the realization of F1 of Southern French nasal vowels. *Journal of Phonetics*, **63**, 87–105.

Carignan, C., Shosted, R., Shih, C., & Rong, P. (2011). Compensatory articulation in American English nasalized vowels. *Journal of Phonetics*, **39**(4), 668–682.

Chen, M. Y. (1997). Acoustic correlates of English and French nasalized vowels. *The Journal of the Acoustical Society of America*, **102**(4), 2360–2370.

Chen, M. Y., & Wang, W. (1975). Sound change: Actuation and implementation. *Language*, **51**(2), 255–281.

Cho, T., & Ladefoged, P. (1999). Variation and universals in VOT: Evidence from 18 languages. *Journal of Phonetics*, **27**(2), 207–229.

Cho, T., Kim, D., & Kim, S. (2017). Prosodically-conditioned fine-tuning of coarticulatory vowel nasalization in English. *Journal of Phonetics*, **64**, 71–89.

Chomsky, N., & Halle, M. (1968). *The Sound Pattern of English*. New York: Harper & Row.

Clayards, M., Tanenhaus, M. K., Aslin, R. N., & Jacobs, R. A. (2008). Perception of speech reflects optimal use of probabilistic speech cues. *Cognition*, **108**(3), 804–809.

Cohn, A. C. (1990). Phonetic and phonological rules of nasalization. Doctoral dissertation, University of California, Los Angeles.

Cohn, A. C., & Renwick, M. E. (2021). Embracing multidimensionality in phonological analysis. *The Linguistic Review*, **38**(1), 101–139.

De Jong, K. J. (1995). The supraglottal articulation of prominence in English: Linguistic stress as localized hyperarticulation. *The Journal of the Acoustical Society of America*, **97**(1), 491–504.

De Jong, K. (2004). Stress, lexical focus, and segmental focus in English: Patterns of variation in vowel duration. *Journal of Phonetics*, **32**(4), 493–516.

De Jong, N. H., Wempe, T., Quené, H., and Persoon, I. (2017). Praat Script Speech Rate V2. https://sites.google.com/site/speechrate/Home/praat-script-syllable-nuclei-v2.

Delvaux, V., Demolin, D., Harmegnies, B., & Soquet, A. (2008). The aerodynamics of nasalization in French. *Journal of Phonetics*, **36**(4), 578–606.

Demolin, D. (2007). Coarticulatory timing and aerodynamics of nasals and nasalization. In *Proceedings of the 16th International Congress of Phonetic Sciences (ICPhS 2007)*, pp. 271–274.

Farnetani, E. (1990). VCV lingual coarticulation and its spatiotemporal domain. In W. J. Hardcastle and A. Marchal, eds., *Speech Production and Speech Modelling*. Dordrecht: Springer, pp. 93–130.

Fowler, C. A. (2005). Parsing coarticulated speech in perception: Effects of coarticulation resistance. *Journal of Phonetics*, **33**(2), 199–213.

Garellek, M., Ritchart, A., & Kuang, J. (2016). Breathy voice during nasality: A cross-linguistic study. *Journal of Phonetics*, **59**, 110–121.

Hajek, J. (1997). *Universals of Sound Change in Nasalization*, vol. 31. Oxford: Blackwell.

Hajek, J. (2013). Vowel nasalization. In M. Dryer and M. Haspelmath, eds., *The World Atlas of Language Structures Online*. Leipzig: Max Planck Institute for Evolutionary Anthropology. http://wals.info/chapter/10, accessed on May 30, 2021.

Hajek, J., & Maeda, S. (2000). Investigating universals of sound change: The effect of vowel height and duration on the development of distinctive nasalization. *Papers in Laboratory Phonology V: Acquisition and the Lexicon*. Cambridge: Cambridge University Press, pp. 52–69.

Harrington, J., Kleber, F., & Reubold, U. (2013). The effect of prosodic weakening on the production and perception of trans-consonantal vowel coarticulation in German. *The Journal of the Acoustical Society of America*, **134**(1), 551–561.

Huffman, M. K. 1988. Timing of contextual nasalization in two languages. *UCLA Working Papers in Phonetics*, **69**, 68–76.

Jackobson, R., Fant, G., & Halle, M. (1952). *Preliminaries to Speech Analysis: The Distinctive Features*. Cambridge: MIT Press.

Jang, J., Kim, S., & Cho, T. (2018). Focus and boundary effects on coarticulatory vowel nasalization in Korean with implications for cross-linguistic similarities and differences. *The Journal of the Acoustical Society of America*, **144**(1), EL33–EL39.

Kawasaki, H. (1986). Phonetic explanation for phonological universals: The case of distinctive vowel nasalization. In J. J. Ohala and J. J. Jaeger, eds., *Experimental Phonology*. New York: Academic Press, pp. 81–103.

Keating, P. A., & Cohn, A. C. (1988). Cross-language effects of vowels on consonant onsets. *The Journal of the Acoustical Society of America*, **84**(S1), S84–S84.

Kenstowicz, M., & Kisseberth, C. (2014). *Generative Phonology: Description and Theory*. New York: Academic Press.

Kleinschmidt, D. F., & Jaeger, T. F. (2015). Robust speech perception: Recognize the familiar, generalize to the similar, and adapt to the novel. *Psychological Review*, **122**(2), 148–203.

Krakow, R. A., & Beddor, P. S. (1991). Coarticulation and the perception of nasality. In *Proceedings of the 12th International Congress of Phonetic Sciences (ICPhS 1991)*, pp. 38–41.

Krakow, R. A., Beddor, P. S., Goldstein, L. M., & Fowler, C. A. (1988). Coarticulatory influences on the perceived height of nasal vowels. *The Journal of the Acoustical Society of America*, **83**(3), 1146–1158.

Kraljic, T., & Samuel, A. G. (2006). Generalization in perceptual learning for speech. *Psychonomic Bulletin & Review*, **13**(2), 262–268.

Kuznetsova, A., Brockhoff, P. B., & Christensen, R. H. (2017). lmerTest package: Tests in linear mixed effects models. *Journal of Statistical Software*, **82**(13), 1–26.

Ladefoged, P. (1971). *Preliminaries to Linguistic Phonetics*. Chicago: University of Chicago Press.

Lahiri, A., & Marslen-Wilson, W. (1991). The mental representation of lexical form: A phonological approach to the recognition lexicon. *Cognition*, **38**(3), 245–294.

Lindblom, B. (1990). Explaining phonetic variation: A sketch of the H&H theory. In W. J. Hardcastle and A. Marchal, eds., *Speech Production and Speech Modelling*. Dordrecht: Springer, pp. 403–439.

Lindblom, B., Guion, S., Hura, S., Moon, S. J., & Willerman, R. (1995). Is sound change adaptive?. *Rivista di Linguistica*, **7**, 5–36.

Maddieson, I. (2013). Absence of Common Consonants. In M. Dryer and M. Haspelmath, eds., *The World Atlas of Language Structures* Online. Leipzig: Max Planck Institute for Evolutionary Anthropology. http://wals .info/chapter/18, accessed on May 30, 2021.

Manuel, S. Y. (1990). The role of contrast in limiting vowel-to-vowel coarticulation in different languages. *The Journal of the Acoustical Society of America*, **88**(3), 1286–1298.

Manuel, S. (1999). Cross-language studies: Relating language-particular coarticulation patterns to other language-particular facts. In W. J. Hardcastle and N. Hewlett, eds., *Coarticulation: Theory, Data and Techniques*. Cambridge: Cambridge University Press, pp. 179–198.

Manuel, S. Y., & Krakow, R. A. (1984). Universal and language particular aspects of vowel-to-vowel coarticulation. *Haskins Laboratories Status Report on Speech Research*, **77**(78), 69–78.

Matisoff, J. A. (1975). Rhinoglottophilia: The mysterious connection between nasality and glottality. In C. A. Ferguson, L. M. Hyman, and J. J. Ohala, eds., *Nasálfest: Papers from a Symposium on Nasals and Nasalization*. Palo Alto, CA: Stanford University Language Universals Project, pp. 265–287.

McMurray, B., & Jongman, A. (2011). What information is necessary for speech categorization? Harnessing variability in the speech signal by integrating cues computed relative to expectations. *Psychological Review*, **118**(2), 219–246.

McMurray, B., Tanenhaus, M. K., & Aslin, R. N. (2002). Gradient effects of within-category phonetic variation on lexical access. *Cognition*, **86**(2), B33–B42.

Merrifield, W. R. (1963). Palantla Chinantec syllable types. *Anthropological Linguistics*, 1–16.

Merrifield, W. R., & Edmondson, J. A. (1999). Palantla Chinantec: Phonetic experiments on nasalization, stress, and tone. *International Journal of American Linguistics*, **65**(3), 303–323.

Miller, J. L., & Volaitis, L. E. (1989). Effect of speaking rate on the perceptual structure of a phonetic category. *Perception & Psychophysics*, **46**(6), 505–512.

Moon, S. J., & Lindblom, B. (1994). Interaction between duration, context, and speaking style in English stressed vowels. *The Journal of the Acoustical Society of America*, **96**(1), 40–55.

Montagu, J., & Amelot, A. (2005). Comparaison des apports de différentes méthodes d'enregistrement de la nasalité. In *Rencontre Jeunes Chercheurs*. Toulouse: Université Paul Sabatier, pp. 17–21.

Munson, B., & Solomon, N. P. (2004). The effect of phonological neighborhood density on vowel articulation. *Journal of Speech, Language, and Hearing Research*, **47**(5), 1048–1058.

Ohala, J. J. (1974). Experimental historical phonology. In J. M. Anderson and C. Jones, eds., *Historical Linguistics*, vol. 2. Amsterdam: North-Holland, pp. 353–389.

Ohala, J. J. (1975). Phonetic explanations for nasal sound patterns. In C. A. Ferguson, L. M. Hyman, and J. J. Ohala, eds., *Nasálfest: Papers from a Symposium on Nasals and Nasalization*. Palo Alto, CA: Stanford University Language Universals Project, pp. 289–316.

Ohala, J. J. (1993). Coarticulation and phonology. *Language and Speech*, **36**(2–3), 155–170.

Ohala, J. J., & Ohala, M. (1995). Speech perception and lexical representation: The role of vowel nasalization in Hindi and English. In B. Connell and A. Arvaniti, eds., *Phonology and Phonetic Evidence*. Cambridge: Cambridge University Press, pp. 41–60.

Picheny, M. A., Durlach, N. I., & Braida, L. D. (1985). Speaking clearly for the hard of hearing I: Intelligibility differences between clear and conversational speech. *Journal of Speech, Language, and Hearing Research*, **28**(1), 96–103.

Pierrehumbert, J. B. 2002. Word-specific phonetics. In C. Gussenhoven and N. Warner, eds., *Laboratory phonology VII*. Berlin: Mouton de Gruyter, pp. 101–140.

Pierrehumbert, J. B. (2016). Phonological representation: Beyond abstract versus episodic. *Annual Review of Linguistics*, **2**, 33–52.

Rosenfelder, I., Fruehwald, J., Evanini, K., & Yuan, J. (2011). FAVE (forced alignment and vowel extraction) program suite.

Ruhlen, M. (1978). Nasal vowels. In J. H. Greenberg, ed., *Universals of Human Language*. Stanford, CA: Stanford University Press, pp. 1–36.

Sampson, R. (1999). *Nasal vowel evolution in Romance*. Oxford: Oxford University Press.

Scarborough, R. A. (2004). Coarticulation and the structure of the lexicon. Doctoral dissertation, University of California, Los Angeles.

Scarborough, R. (2012). Lexical similarity and speech production: Neighborhoods for nonwords. *Lingua*, **122**(2), 164–176.

Scarborough, R. (2013). Neighborhood-conditioned patterns in phonetic detail: Relating coarticulation and hyperarticulation. *Journal of Phonetics*, **41**(6), 491–508.

Scarborough, R., & Zellou, G. (2013). Clarity in communication: "Clear" speech authenticity and lexical neighborhood density effects in speech production and perception. *The Journal of the Acoustical Society of America*, **134**(5), 3793–3807.

Scarborough, R., Zellou, G., Mirzayan, A., & Rood, D. S. (2015). Phonetic and phonological patterns of nasality in Lakota vowels. *Journal of the International Phonetic Association*, **45**(3), 289–309.

Schourup, L. (1973). A cross-language study of vowel nasal coarticulation. *Ohio State University Working Papers in Linguistics*, **15**, 190–221.

Solé, M. J. (1992). Phonetic and phonological processes: The case of nasalization. *Language and Speech*, **35**(1–2), 29–43.

Solé, M. J. (1995). Spatio-temporal patterns of velopharyngeal action in phonetic and phonological nasalization. *Language and Speech*, **38**(1), 1–23.

Solé, M. J. (2007). Controlled and mechanical properties in speech. In M.-J. Solé, P. S. Beddor, and J. J. Ohala, eds., *Experimental Approaches to Phonology*. Oxford: Oxford University Press, pp. 302–321.

Smiljanić, R., & Bradlow, A. R. (2009). Speaking and hearing clearly: Talker and listener factors in speaking style changes. *Language and Linguistics Compass*, **3**(1), 236–264.

Stoakes, H. M., Fletcher, J. M., & Butcher, A. R. (2020). Nasal coarticulation in Bininj Kunwok: An aerodynamic analysis. *Journal of the International Phonetic Association*, **50**(3), 305–332.

Styler, W. (2017). On the acoustical features of vowel nasality in English and French. *The Journal of the Acoustical Society of America*, **142**(4), 2469–2482.

Tamminga, M., & Zellou, G. (2015). Cross-dialectal differences in nasal coarticulation in American English. In *Proceedings of the 18th International Congress of Phonetic Sciences (ICPhS 2015)*, pp. 1–4.

Tamminga, M., Wilder, R., Lai, W., & Wade, L. (2020). Perceptual learning, talker specificity, and sound change. *Papers in Historical Phonology*, **5**, 90–122.

Toscano, J. C., McMurray, B., Dennhardt, J., & Luck, S. J. (2010). Continuous perception and graded categorization: Electrophysiological evidence for a linear relationship between the acoustic signal and perceptual encoding of speech. *Psychological Science*, **21**(10), 1532–1540.

Warren, P., & Marslen-Wilson, W. (1987). Continuous uptake of acoustic cues in spoken word recognition. *Perception & Psychophysics*, **41**(3), 262–275.

Weinreich, U., Labov, W., & Herzog, M. (1968). *Empirical Foundations for a Theory of Language Change.* Austin: University of Texas Press.

Wetzels, W. L., & Nevins, A. (2018). Prenasalized and postoralized consonants: The diverse functions of enhancement. *Language,* **94**(4), 834–866.

Wright, J. T. (1986). The behavior of nasalized vowels in the perceptual vowel space. In J. J. Ohala and J. J. Jaeger, eds., *Experimental Phonology.* New York: Academic Press, pp 45–67.

Wright, R. (2004). Factors of lexical competition in vowel articulation. *Papers in Laboratory Phonology* VI, 75–87.

Yu, A. C. (2010). Perceptual compensation is correlated with individuals' "autistic" traits: Implications for models of sound change. *PloS one,* **5**(8), e11950.

Yu, A. C., & Zellou, G. (2019). Individual differences in language processing: Phonology. *Annual Review of Linguistics,* **5,** 131–150.

Zellou, G. (2017). Individual differences in the production of nasal coarticulation and perceptual compensation. *Journal of Phonetics,* **61,** 13–29.

Zellou, G., & Brotherton, C. (2021). Phonetic imitation of multidimensional acoustic variation of the nasal split short-a system. *Speech Communication,* **135,** 54–65.

Zellou, G., & Dahan, D. (2019). Listeners maintain phonological uncertainty over time and across words: The case of vowel nasality in English. *Journal of Phonetics,* **76,** 100910.

Zellou, G., & Ferenc Segedin, B. (2019). The distribution of coarticulatory variation influences perceptual adaptation. In *Proceedings of the 19th International Congress of Phonetic Sciences (ICPhS 2019),* pp. 393–397.

Zellou, G., & Scarborough, R. (2012). Nasal Coarticulation and Contrastive Stress. In *Proceedings of the Thirteenth Annual Conference of the International Speech Communication Association,* pp. 2686–2689.

Zellou, G., & Scarborough, R. (2015). Lexically conditioned phonetic variation in motherese: age-of-acquisition and other word-specific factors in infant- and adult-directed speech. *Laboratory Phonology,* **6**(3–4), 305–336.

Zellou, G., & Scarborough, R. (2019). Neighborhood-conditioned phonetic enhancement of an allophonic vowel split. *The Journal of the Acoustical Society of America,* **145**(6), 3675–3685.

Zellou, G., & Tamminga, M. (2014). Nasal coarticulation changes over time in Philadelphia English. *Journal of Phonetics,* **47,** 18–35.

Zellou, G., Dahan, D., & Embick, D. (2017). Imitation of coarticulatory vowel nasality across words and time. *Language, Cognition and Neuroscience*, **32**(6), 776–791.

Zellou, G., Scarborough, R., & Nielsen, K. (2016). Phonetic imitation of coarticulatory vowel nasalization. *The Journal of the Acoustical Society of America*, **140**(5), 3560–3575.

Acknowledgments

Many thanks to editor Patrycja Strycharczuk and two anonymous reviewers for their helpful comments and feedback.